D. James Kennedy

Learning to Live with the People You Love

LEARNING TO LIVE WITH THE PEOPLE YOU LOVE

D. James Kennedy, Ph.D.

Copyright © 1987 by D. James Kennedy
Printed in the United States of America
ISBN: 0-88368-190-0

Compiled and edited by Valeria Cindric.

Unless otherwise noted, Bible quotations are taken from the *King James Version*.

Scripture quotations marked *NIV* are from the Holy Bible, *New International Version*. Copyright © 1973, 1978, International Bible Society. Used by permission.

Scripture quotations marked *TLB* are from *The Living Bible*. Copyright © 1971 by Tyndale House Publishers, Wheaton, Illinois. Used by permission.

Poems quoted in this book are taken from *Your Marriage: Duel or Duet?* by Dr. Louis Evans. Copyright © 1962 and used by permission.

Material quoted from *Marriage: The Mystery of Christ and the Church* by David Englesma, copyright © 1975, is used with permission from Reformed Free Publishing Association, Grand Rapids, Michigan.

All rights reserved. No portion of this book may be used without written permission of the publisher, with the exception of brief excerpts in magazine articles, reviews, etc. For further information or permission, address Whitaker House, Pittsburgh & Colfax Streets, Springdale, Pennsylvania 15144.

CONTENTS

DEDICATION

This book is affectionately dedicated to my wife Anne and our daughter Jennifer, who have made it easy for me to learn to live with the people I love.

THE TREASURES IN YOUR BACKYARD

In the book, *Acres of Diamonds,* Russell H. Conwell recalls the story of a prosperous Persian man who left his family and sold his property to go in search of diamonds. His search, however, was in vain, ending in poverty and death. But the farmer who had bought his land found acres of diamonds lying in the fields behind the house. This discovery unearthed some of the world's largest diamonds and produced one of the most magnificent diamond mines in history. The treasure sought by the first man had belonged to him all along; he just never knew it.

What do you see when you look into your backyard? The children playing on the swingset? Your husband mowing the lawn? Your wife weeding the flower garden? Could these loved ones possibly hold the key to the treasure you have been seeking?

The Bible tells us that the true treasure of life can be found in *relationships*—with God and with people. God has placed us in families so we can discover in our earthly relationships something of that special treasure found only in heaven above.

Most of us would say, "I love my spouse and family." That may be, but building relationships is more than saying, "I love you." It is sharing life together in a way that brings glory to God and enriches the lives of every family member.

Let's look at how you can learn to live with the people you love—and discover life's richest treasures within the boundaries of your own backyard.

Part One

LEARNING TO LIVE
WITH YOUR SPOUSE

1

CAPTURING THE
BIRD OF PARADISE

On a recent television program a handsome young man was talking to an older man about whether or not he should get married. After a number of comments concerning the young lady in question, the older man finally asked, "Do you love her?"

The young man replied, "Oh yes! I'm madly in love with her."

"Then by all means marry her," said the older man.

Most people conceive of love as a *feeling* that is like a mysterious bird of paradise. We do not know where it comes from, why it comes to some, or why it leaves others. But somehow this mysterious bird flaps its wings, floats down on two people, and they are "in love." What a glorious, marvelous experience!

When two people "fall in love," they often get married. Then two years later, they wake up one morning and decide the bird has flown away and taken paradise with it. No one knows why, but the bird has gone; and the once-happy couple has "fallen out of love." So they get divorced and wander through life, waiting and hoping the mysterious bird will descend from the skies and once again bring them a touch of paradise.

This secular view of marriage has created devastating consequences. Statistics indicate that one out of two marriages in America ends in divorce. That means the chances of remaining in paradise are only fifty-fifty—very discouraging odds for any venture, much less one that can leave permanent scars and a long trail of heartache.

I read in a magazine about a Hollywood actress who was getting married because she was *in love*. This time she believed it was going to work because she was *really* in love. The other three times she *thought* she was in love, but she had been wrong. This time she was *sure*.

This flaky view of romantic love has penetrated the church to an alarming degree, and the result is an increasing number of divorces among Christians. I have counseled young couples who, before they were married, boldly professed their love and made assertions of an undying concern for one another. After two years of marriage, I have seen them axing one another to death in a divorce court. What happened to the undying love that was going to last until the stars burned out and the mountains fell into the sea?

Romantic Love

Most people would say that *love and romance* are the foundation of any successful marriage. This is a beautiful sentiment, but it is not true. In fact, many marital problems result from an erroneous concept of what love is.

Dr. John W. Drakeford, in his book, *How to Keep A Good Thing Going*, describes the characteristics of *romantic love*. He says that being in love is preeminently an experience of the emotions that causes irrational behavior and often immobilizes its victims. No wonder so many marriages fail.

Some of the confusion about love comes from the different ways the word is used in the English language. "I love my new Honda." "I love baseball." "I love your hairdo." "I love chocolate."

Remember the song that says, "What the world needs now is love, sweet love"? The world quickly adopted the songwriter's ideas, and now we have more "free love" than ever before—or free sex, as it should be called. Many people use the word love when they really mean lust or sex.

The word "love" is also used to describe the feeling of infatuation or what we call "puppy love"—so named because it lasts about as long as a puppy remains a puppy. Unfortunately, many couples get married on the basis of infatuation and then wonder why their love doesn't last until the puppy is grown. "Infatuation" comes from the Latin word *infatuare* whose root meaning also forms the English word "foolish." Anyone who builds a relationship, especially their marriage, on infatuation is foolish indeed.

When I was a teenager, I often sang these words from a popular song: "Will I ever find the girl on my mind, the one who is my ideal? Or will I pass her by and never even know that she was my ideal?" Today, I'm wise enough to know—*that* is a bunch of hogwash! Many single people delude themselves into thinking that if they find that one soulmate—Mr. or Miss Right—then they will experience the pitter-patter in their heart, hear the flip-flap of the bird of paradise, and sail off into the sunset.

Reality, however, portrays a different scenario. When one spouse or the other loses the feeling of love, the bird falls like a dead owl, and someone is left out on a limb all alone.

Learning To Love

This *feeling* that people call love is not what the Bible means by love at all. According to Scripture, love is not a feeling; *love is a way of acting.* True love, as God's Word tells us, is *a way of treating other people.* Notice in the following Scripture passage that there is not one tingle of emotion—not even a palpitation!

> Love is patient, love is kind. It does not envy,
> it does not boast, it is not proud. It is not rude,
> it is not self-seeking, it is not easily angered, it
> keeps no record of wrongs. Love does not delight
> in evil but rejoices with the truth. It always

protects, always trusts, always hopes, always perseveres—1 Corinthians 13:4-7, *NIV.*

When a young man and woman are dating, they are extremely patient and kind with one another. They never say anything rude or demand their own way. Angry words and actions are seldom exhibited. They defend each other and trust one another explicitly. What happens, then, when these same two people get married? Why do their actions change?

For thousands of years (and in some eastern countries today), the majority of marriages were arranged by parents. The young people involved sometimes never saw each other until their wedding day.

A young lady from India was to be married to a young man whom she had never met. One day she received a letter from her fiance in which he tried to begin a relationship and get acquainted prior to the wedding. The young woman, however, returned the letter unopened, saying she believed love should be developed after marriage and not before. In explaining her view, this young Indian woman said, "When we are born, we cannot choose who will be our mother and father, or our brothers and sisters. Yet we learn to live with them and to love them. So it is with our husband or wife."

In societies where this philosophy is accepted, divorce is almost nonexistent. I am not suggesting we go back to the practice of arranged marriages, but I am saying that romantic love has little to do with a successful marriage relationship.

If two complete strangers meet and treat one another according to 1 Corinthians thirteen, after a while the *feeling* of love will also come. On the other hand, no matter how crazy head-over-heels in love you have fallen with someone, if he or she violates the love principles in God's Word, romantic love will fly out the window—and so will the feeling.

Love, according to the Bible's definition, involves two aspects: *doing* and *enduring*. We can understand this better by looking at Jesus Christ. The life of Christ is divided by theologians into two parts: *His active obedience* and *His passive obedience.*

The *active obedience* of Jesus was everything He *did:* Jesus went about doing good. He healed the sick; He fed the hungry; He forgave the sinner; He comforted the mourner. Christ's *passive obedience* (from which we get the word passion) involves the things He *endured:* mockery, insults, betrayal, injustice, emotional turmoil, sorrow, physical pain, separation from His heavenly Father. Jesus Christ was the perfect embodiment of love as it is defined in 1 Corinthians thirteen. Doing good and enduring evil—that is what love is all about.

A Rose By Any Other Name

Some time ago a lady came to me and said, "I don't love my husband anymore, and I haven't loved him for a long time. There is no love in our home. I think we should get a divorce."

"I am sorry to hear that," I replied. "Tell me about it. Did you ever love him?"

"Oh yes. When I married him, I loved him very much. He was so kind and considerate. But after we were married, he became indifferent toward me. Then he started treating me badly and saying nasty things to me, until I lost all love for him." She paused a moment and then continued, "You know, some years ago I was very sick and had an operation. While I was in the hospital, my husband brought me flowers and candy, sat on the bed, held my hand, and read to me. It's the strangest thing, but I began to love him again at that time."

"Oh, really?" I asked.

"Yes, but it didn't last. After I got out of the hospital, it wasn't long before he was ignoring me again. I haven't felt

13

any love for him in years. So there's nothing left to do. Don't you agree that I should get a divorce?"

"I'll tell you what the Bible says you should do. If you don't love your husband, if you haven't loved him for years, then you should go home, get down on your knees, repent of your sin, and ask the Lord and your husband to forgive you."

She didn't reply, but I've never seen a more shocked expression on anyone's face!

Love isn't an "I hope so" or "I wish I could" or "Maybe I will." *Love is a command:* "See that ye love one another with a pure heart fervently" (1 Peter 1:22). "He has given us this command: Whoever loves God must also love his brother" (1 John 4:21, *NIV*).

If you don't love your husband or wife, you are disobeying God and you need to repent of that sin. "But how can I love him (or her) when I don't feel like it?" You can't command a feeling, but you *can* command your mouth to speak lovingly to your spouse; you *can* make your hands touch with tenderness; you *can* decide to be patient and kind.

If I were to say, "A rose is a delightful aroma, a lovely fragrance." You would say, "No, that is not quite right. A rose is a flower, and it produces a fragrance. But the aroma isn't the flower." When we *do* what 1 Corinthians thirteen says, one of the by-products is the feeling that people call love—the fragrance. But the love—the real rose—is what we do and what we endure for one another.

Love—like a rose—is very delicate and needs to be handled gently. Anyone who has ever had a rose garden knows that beautiful flowers do not happen naturally. Roses require a great deal of work and attention. You can keep the fragrance in your marriage by carefully nourishing and caring for the love that is there. How about your marriage? Has the once sweet-smelling rose turned brown around the edges and lost not only its fragrance but its beauty?

The love the Bible talks about doesn't come naturally for fallen man. Because of our selfish, sinful nature, we do not have it within us to love. Love is supernatural: "God is love" (1 John 4:16).

How, then, can we ever experience love? God has given us the Holy Spirit, and one of the fruits of the Spirit is love. (See Galatians 5:22.) If you try to love your husband or wife but ignore God—the fountain and source of all love—you will find yourself chasing an illusive rainbow. If, however, you seek God with all your heart and ask Him to fill you with His Spirit of love, a miracle will occur in your heart and in your marriage.

Heavenly Father, teach us how to love one another. Forgive us for our misconceptions and ignorance about what love really is. By the power of Your Holy Spirit, help us to love our spouses with the love of Jesus and by the principles established in Your Word. In Jesus' name. Amen.

2

WHY PEOPLE GET MARRIED

Why do people get married? To have someone to take care of them? To legalize their living arrangement? To have children and a family? For security and companionship in their old age?

If you observed the habits and conduct of many American marriages, you would conclude that one of these ideas must be the reason behind this institution. But what is *God's* purpose in having two people marry?

Long before God established the church, the state, or the school, He created marriage. The goal for this God-ordained institution is clearly set forth for us in Scripture—first mentioned in Genesis, it is later repeated several times in the New Testament: *"They shall be one."* (See Genesis 2:24, Matthew 19:6, Mark 10:8.)

Oneness is God's purpose for marriage. Yet most of us have only dimly perceived the supreme goal God intends for a husband and wife to achieve. In fact, most couples do not have any concept of what they are trying to accomplish in their marriage.

The oneness designed for marriage partners is compared to the relationship believers share with Christ. In this ''mystical union,'' Christ, the bridegroom, joins Himself to His bride, the Church; and they become *one*. In this oneness with Christ, man enjoys his highest spiritual communion. On earth, God intends for us to enjoy a similar union in marriage. (See Ephesians 5:23-33.)

Some people say that marriage is a fifty-fifty partnership. Others say, "No, it is not fifty-fifty; it is a 100 percent partnership." According to Christ, marriage is not a partnership at all; it is a *relationship*. Marriage is the closest relationship any two people can know in this world. Even the relationship between parent and child does not involve the same kind of oneness that a husband and wife enjoy.

God's Purpose For Marriage

To understand God's original purpose for marriage, we must go back to the Garden of Eden. God placed Adam in that perfect environment and provided for his every possible need. Anything he desired was available to him for the taking; he simply had to pluck it off a tree. This man whom God created was the epitome of humanity—physically perfect with a superior intellect.

Yet, when God looked upon Adam—with his tremendous mental capacities, his physical prowess, his perfect environment, his spiritual communion with the Creator—He found man lacking. God said, "It is not good that the man should be alone" (Genesis 2:18).

The singles movement in America today says, "God, you are wrong. It *is* good for man to be alone. It's really cool!" Even married people accept the current fads of modern society and go their own way, never realizing that the deepest, most fulfilling spiritual union that can be experienced with another human being is found in marriage.

Although Adam enjoyed the companionship of beautiful horses, lovable lions, and cuddly lambs, he did not have a suitable helper. None of the animals could meet Adam's needs, so the Creator designed a completely new being for man. God put Adam into a deep sleep, took one of his ribs, and out of that rib built a woman. The writer of Genesis does not use the word "create" or "fashion" as he had previously, but he writes that God "built" a woman.

How did Adam respond when God presented this new created being to him? "This is it!" Adam exclaimed. "She is part of my own bone and flesh! Her name is 'woman' because she was taken out of man" (Genesis 2:23, *TLB*). Adam and Eve enjoyed a perfect oneness that no other couple will ever experience. They were literally one flesh—made from the same body.

God designated this oneness when He called *their* name "Adam." (See Genesis 5:1.) This concept is contrary to the modern thinking of the liberated woman who wants to maintain her independence. She balks at being called the "Adamses" and instead keeps her maiden name to prove she is a separate individual.

When a man and woman get married, they are no more two but one flesh. Although they are not made from the same body, as Adam and Eve were, there is a unique oneness between husband and wife that no other human relationship enjoys. Husbands, *your wife is you*! Wives, *your husband is you*! If you can grasp this fact and hold onto it, your marriage will never be the same.

Cutting Off Your Head

God said that a husband and wife are *indissolubly one*—one flesh. Could you rip off your arm or tear off your leg? No wonder God said He hates divorce. *Divorce violently wrenches apart that which is meant to be inseparable.* "What therefore God has joined together, let not man put asunder" (Matthew 19:6).

When you get a cold and have a runny nose, watery eyes, and ringing ears, you try many remedies in an effort to alleviate your suffering. But one solution is never contemplated—cutting off your head! The Bible says the husband is the head of the household. Wives, you may have trouble with your husband, and he may be doing things that displease you; but the answer is not to cut off your head.

Husbands, if you are having problems in your marriage, the solution is not to cut out your heart—the wife who loves you.

Once couples realize that the husband/wife relationship is permanent, solutions other than cutting off the undesirable partner will be considered. Most of the problems in marriage start because couples regard their relationship as some sort of probationary experiment that, if it works out, fine; if not, that's too bad—"We tried." They view marriage as a temporary arrangement with a ninety-day, money-back guarantee: 'til the divorce court doth us part; 'til the mid-life crisis doth us part. God, however, designed marriage to be a *permanent relationship*—'til *death* do you part.

Married couples need to commit themselves to fulfilling the vows they made on their wedding day. The Bible says it is a grievous and heinous sin to break a vow, and God is greatly displeased with those who do so. "When you make a vow to God, do not delay in fulfilling it. He has no pleasure in fools; fulfill your vow" (Ecclesiastes 5:4, *NIV*). We need to have this same attitude toward our marriage vows. Divorce is not a viable option to marital problems. Commit yourself to the permanence of your marriage, and don't even mention the word divorce in your home.

Marriage is built on *commitment*—"for better or worse, in sickness and in health." When a man and woman commit themselves for life to one another, they will *not* have a footnote in the back of their mind that says, "If things get really tough, I'll check out."

Husbands and wives who do not see their marriage as an irrevocable, indissoluble, and permanent union will never experience the oneness that Christ says exists in that special relationship. You may be thinking that this means you are condemned to a life-sentence of misery and heartache. "Oh, he'll never change. He's just like his father." Or, "She'll never be any different. She's just like her mother."

Yet, the whole thrust of the Biblical message is that God *can* change people. When we take the position that our spouse will never change, we are insulting God and His Word. By the power of the Holy Spirit, your spouse can become the husband or wife God wants him or her to be.

God has a plan for improving your marriage. If you commit yourself to discovering how you can implement His perfect will in your marital relationship, your marriage will be a success.

Leaving And Cleaving

The concept of oneness—"They shall be one flesh"— established in the garden of Eden was preceded by a rather unusual statement: "Therefore shall a man leave his father and his mother, and shall cleave to his wife" (Genesis 2:24). What do a person's parents have to do with oneness in marriage?

The wedding ceremony drives a stake into *time,* dividing a person's life into two periods: the time when one is bound to parents and the time when one is bound to husband or wife. That is why "leaving" is so important. If a couple is going to have oneness with their spouse, a leaving of the parents must first take place.

Sometimes a young person says, "Yes, forsaking all others, leaving father and mother, I take this one to be my husband or wife." Yet, once married, they are continually looking over their shoulder at mom and dad. How many husbands and wives have endeavored to remake their spouse in the image of dear old dad or wonderful mom? "That is not the way dad carved the turkey," or "That's not how mom made an apple pie." The husband is tied to his mother's apron strings, and the wife wants nothing less than good old dad in a younger form. A husband or wife who cannot break the parent/child bond will have difficulty establishing true oneness with their marriage partner.

A marriage starts with *leaving,* but it develops with *cleaving.* In Genesis 2:24, the word used for "cleave" refers to the kind of bonding that occurs when two pieces of wood are glued together. Today, it is rare to see couples who exhibit a real cleaving to one another.

I heard a story about a civilian couple who were invited to a military banquet where the husband was to be the keynote speaker. The colonel who had invited them showed the wife where she was to sit. He then began to lead the husband to a seat at the head table. The husband stopped and said, "No, I prefer to sit with my wife."

The colonel replied, "I am sorry, but it is military protocol that you be seated up front."

"I don't care about military protocol. God made us one, and you are trying to separate us. I will sit with my wife." When the people attending the banquet overheard the husband's reply, they stood and applauded.

How is the oneness in your marriage? Do you have two soloists, or do you have a duet? Do you have your own interests, your own friends, your own enjoyments, and your own entertainments? Do you allow the world to pull you apart? Do the two of you go your own ways and occasionally meet at the home refueling center?

If this describes your marriage, then ask God to help you experience the deeper joy, love, and peace that comes with true oneness. "And they shall be one." Make that the goal of your marriage.

This is my prayer for you and your spouse:

Father, may the two in each marriage be made one, even as we have been made one in You through Jesus Christ our Lord. May those who have not known true oneness with Christ reach out the hand of faith and put their trust in Him. May they be cleansed, renewed, and enabled to know the oneness in marriage that You have designed for them to enjoy. May each husband and wife be one flesh in You. In Jesus' name. Amen.

3
THE ESSENCE OF MARRIAGE

A cartoon in the *Wall Street Journal* showed an obviously successful businessman looking over the newspaper at his wife and saying, "I communicate all day long at the office—isn't that enough?" We can imagine what the wife must have said to evoke such a response from her husband. The sad reality of this situation leaves little room for humor. How many wives feel hurt and neglected because communication on their husband's part ends when he walks in the door at night?

Communication is as important in the home as it is at the office—or anywhere else. The sharing of thoughts, dreams, plans, problems, and emotions is essential to oneness in a marital relationship. A well-known marriage counselor says the major complaint made by wives is, "My husband won't communicate with me or listen to me."

Because many couples have never grasped the reality of what marriage is all about, they have experienced little in the way of communication. This is due, in part, to the fact that they see their primary goal in marriage as simply earning a living, making a home, and raising a family. Creating a oneness in their relationship hardly enters their minds.

We've all known marriages where the wife is a chatterbox and the husband is a sphinx. A lot of one-sided talk may take place, but no real communication occurs. The wife complains that her husband doesn't talk to her, but she fails to understand that he can't get a word in edgewise. He's been trying for thirty years and hasn't succeeded yet! So the husband gives up. When the wife wants his opinion, she'll give it to him. When you want to know what the husband thinks, she'll tell you. I know a marriage like this that recently ended in divorce, and the wife was totally oblivious to the real problem.

Many married couples operate with a competitive attitude that says, "Can you top this?" When the husband comes home in the evening, his wife meets him, saying, "What a day I had! The children drove me absolutely wild. I'm so frazzled I can hardly think straight!" What an opportunity for this husband to sympathize with his wife and her situation.

But his response usually is: "Ha! You think you had trouble today. You should have seen it down at that rat race of an office. I mean to tell you the rats were chewing the tails off each other!"

When openness on the part of one spouse is used as an opportunity for ridiculing, scoffing, criticizing, or faultfinding by the other, any kind of deep communication drys up altogether. Marriages often fail because one mate is unwilling to try to meet the needs of the other. Everyone needs to be appreciated, understood, listened to, and respected.

Many couples, if asked, "What are your spouse's greatest aspirations?" would not be able to answer. They cannot identify one another's goals in life, greatest fears, or deepest needs because they never cared enough to ask.

Levels Of Communication

Marriage counselors tell us that the number one problem in marriage is poor communication. "We can never discuss anything without your blowing up or walking out." "Why is it that we can never talk anything out?" "What can we do? It seems so hopeless."

Every couple wants to be able to communicate, but somehow, after trying and trying, they have failed repeatedly.

Many have given up altogether and resigned themselves to a humdrum marriage with little meaningful sharing. Yet, their hearts yearn for a deeper, richer, more intimate relationship with their spouse.

John Powell wrote an interesting book with this thought-provoking title: *Why Am I Afraid To Tell You Who I Am?* Do you share that fear? Many people find it difficult to express their true feelings. Yet it is in the sharing of hearts that a husband and wife are most deeply joined together. How about your marriage? Are feelings freely shared?

Powell has found that people communicate on one or more of five different levels. See if you can determine the level on which you and your spouse usually communicate.

The lowest level of communication is called *cliche conversation.* On this safe level, no personal risks are involved. Husbands and wives often have this type of conversation: "Good morning. How did you sleep? Your breakfast is on the table. Will you stop for milk on the way home? By the way, the car needs gas. Have a nice day. See you later." This kind of communication may be good for starters, but some couples never get beyond this point. When they've exhausted their little group of cliches, they are left speechless and all communication ends.

The next level of communication involves *reporting the facts about others.* Our conversation centers around what we have read, what other people have said, or what someone else has done. "The boss's wife had an operation yesterday. Your mother called while you were out. The weatherman said it's going to rain this afternoon. Johnny got a B in English." No effort is made to offer an opinion or tell how we feel about these issues or events. Gossip is an example of this low level of sharing.

Risky Business

When we can express *our ideas and judgments* about issues and events, real communication begins. At last, the

25

soul steps out of its solitary confinement and begins to share, in a very limited way, its existence with another person. As soon as you begin to express what you think about something or tell what you believe, you are exposing a piece of yourself. This can be risky business.

To avoid dangerous ground, some people act like politicians. "Well, what do you think? . . . That's how I feel about it, too." They don't seem to have any opinions about issues, any beliefs about life, or any new ideas. And if they do, they keep them to themselves. On the other hand, some people are very adept at expressing their judgments and convictions on a broad spectrum of subjects, yet no real communication occurs because it is all one-sided.

A higher level of communication occurs when *feelings and emotions* are honestly expressed. We are not simply sharing something that may have happened (which is a fact), or what we may think about it (which is an opinion), but how we *feel* about it—our hopes, anxieties, and joys. Some people will discuss their feelings about the safe areas of life as long as they don't have to share about things that intimately affect them—like their marriage, their feelings toward their husband or wife, or their attitude toward life.

A missionary couple returned from the foreign field because their marriage was dissolving and their ministry was failing. After discussing all their problems with a counselor, the wife finally blurted out, "I didn't love this man when I married him, and I have never loved him since!" Once these deep, hidden feelings were expressed, the problem areas in their marriage could be dealt with honestly and openly. As a result, the husband and wife developed a beautiful new relationship, and they are back on the mission field, serving and glorifying the Lord.

Overcoming The Risks

Once we are able to share our feelings with our spouse, we are on our way to the highest level of communication.

26

This level requires absolute openness and honesty. Many people, however, find that the risks involved on this very personal level are too great, and they are afraid to venture forth. They have a *fear of being rejected* or repulsed if they bare their souls and share their true feelings. This fear of rejection causes many people to clam up, and feelings go unexpressed. When these emotions are never lovingly brought to the surface, where they can be discussed and resolved, they remain locked up inside the person. Like a splinter buried deep in the skin, these feelings fester and can destroy any hope for an intimate relationship between husband and wife.

Other people have a *fear of being betrayed.* For this reason, openness must always be met with responding loyalty on the part of the listener. Proverbs thirty-one says of the virtuous wife: "The heart of her husband doth safely trust in her, so that he shall have no need of spoil. She will do him good and not evil all the days of her life" (verses 11-12). The same should be true of a righteous husband. If we are not trustworthy, how can we expect our mates to be honest and open with us? It is crucial to a healthy marriage for partners not to betray the confidences shared with one another.

Openness requires a certain degree of vulnerability; and vulnerability can only exist where there is complete trust. A deep marital relationship is built on open honesty. Wife, how do you feel about your husband? Husband, how do you feel about your wife? Would you dare tell them?

Some husbands and wives who try to be loving often fail to speak the truth to their mates. Real feelings are not expressed because they feel it would hurt their partner. Yet, any deep personal relationship is based upon complete honesty with one another. Many marriages never progress to a more intimate level of sharing because so much has been left unsaid. If the truth is presented in a loving and positive manner, it will generally be well received.

If you and your mate are willing to deal constructively and honestly with the deepest feelings of your life, one thing is essential—an opportunity. Husbands and wives should plan and schedule time alone together where communication can develop in an uninterrupted atmosphere of peace and quiet. This may seem impossible on a regular basis, but unless you make the opportunity, your quality of communication will remain on the lowest levels. To reach that peak level of deep emotional sharing, you must make an effort to spend quality time alone with your mate.

You may need to rethink your priorities. Which is more important: your job or your wife? the household or your husband? Set aside time to relax and enjoy being together, sharing ideas and activities. Learn to listen sensitively to your mate's innermost thoughts, fears, and feelings. If your husband or wife has difficulty expressing themselves, then you take the initiative and open up to them first. Soon they will feel free to expose their hopes, dreams, and desires.

The Wall Of Ice

Have you ever tried to communicate with someone only to find yourself talking to a stone wall? As soon as you hit on a sensitive issue or begin sharing on a personal level, the barriers go up and the subject is changed to a less threatening topic. What causes these communication blockers?

One of the most common reasons for blocked communication is *resentment*. Many times a husband or wife tries to communicate with their spouse, but their efforts are blocked by a cold, icy wall of resentment. This wall is built on the memory of some previous hurt, slight, or wound.

Resentment is like an inner thermometer that measures the degree of unforgiveness a person is harboring. Are you a resentful person? If so, then you are not a forgiving person. God's Word says to be "tenderhearted, forgiving one another, even as God for Christ's sake hath forgiven you" (Ephesians 4:32). Once you learn to forgive your spouse, the lines of communication will be unclogged, and times of tender sharing will become more frequent.

Jay Adams, a well-known Christian psychologist, in his book, *Christian Living In The Home*, tells about a couple, Sue and Wilbur, who came for counseling. As they sat across the desk from the marriage counselor, Wilbur shifted nervously from one side of his chair to the other.

Sue sat stiffly with her arms folded defiantly and said, "I am not here because I want to be. My physician told me to come. I have an ulcer that is killing me, and he says it is not caused by any physical reason." As she spoke, she reached down into her shopping-bag-sized purse and pulled out an inch-thick manuscript—each page typed single-spaced on both sides. She slapped the document down on the desk and said, "That's why I am here!"

The counselor picked it up to see what it was. When he opened the manuscript, he saw a careful documentation of every slight, every hurt, every word, every deed that Wilbur had committed against his wife for the past thirteen years. (In subsequent visits, this proved to be a very accurate account of their married life.)

"That's what is giving me ulcers!" Sue explained.

The counselor said, "I want you to know, young lady, that it has been many years since I have met anyone" (Sue began to smile, and Wilbur slid further down in his seat) "as hostile and resentful as you are!" With that, Wilbur sat up a little straighter, and the counselor continued, "This is a record, not only of the faults your husband has committed against you, but also of the sin you have committed against him, against God, and against your own body, for which you are now paying a price."

God's Word says that love "keeps no record of wrongs" (1 Corinthians 13:5, *NIV*). You may be wondering how anyone could be so petty as to write down every slight done to them. Some people, however, have extraordinary memories and don't need a notebook to record hurtful incidents. They can cite places, dates, circumstances, and quote dialogue verbatim from years ago. Do you know someone like that? Do you live with that kind of person? Are you one of these I'll-never-forget people?

Sometimes our resentment comes out unexpectedly in little slips of the tongue: "You always do . . . " Obviously, quite a memory tape is being played back in our minds. "Why, you never . . ." Never? That conclusion requires the amassing of a tremendous amount of data. Maybe we are not much different from that young lady with the manuscript after all.

Breakdowns In Communication

Another block to communication is a poor *self-image*. Many people who begin life with a low self-esteem have this image reinforced by others who criticize them, ignore them, make fun of them, and pooh-pooh their ideas. After a while they are convinced that they have nothing to offer; they are not worthwhile; nobody wants to hear what they have to say; and certainly no one cares how they feel. As a result, they learn to withhold their opinions, their ideas, and their personal feelings. This breakdown in communication affects all their relationships.

Do you contribute to a poor self-image in your spouse? Many husbands continually put their wives down by being sarcastic and uninterested in their ideas. Men who treat their wives th● way will find themselves isolated from any form of meaningful communication.

Some wives destroy their husband's self-esteem by trying to usurp the leadership role in the home. She often snaps, "Are you a man or a mouse? Squeak up!" The last big decision she let him make was whether to wash or dry. A put-down is a good way to put off effective communication.

Author Jay Adams says that one of the most common blocks to communication is faultfinding. Instead of dealing with the problem in their marriage, a husband and wife will begin to attack each other. "If you wouldn't do this, it wouldn't be that way!" "Well, you think I am . . . " "What about the way you . . . ?" "Yes, but you always . . . " The problem gets lost in the personal battle that ensues. Instead of focusing on the issue at hand, couples get sidetracked by resentment, hostility, and faultfinding.

Some people think the most important part of a discussion is fixing the blame on the guilty party. They think their calling in life is to be a Colombo or a Sherlock Holmes. Are you a blame fixer? Blamefixing destroys any possibility of creative problem solving. It is also a great and impassable barrier to good communication in a marriage. If couples would focus on the problem and not on each other's faults, they could find a solution to their marital difficulties.

Barking On The Inside

Communication can be blocked by two opposite, yet equally destructive, reactions—*blowing up* and *clamming up.* Some people do both.

The Bible says to "be angry, and sin not" (Ephesians 4:26). When a husband or wife blows up in anger, all sorts of vicious speech is spewed forth. They rile against their mate and tell them off in no uncertain terms. An explosion like that is definitely sin. Nothing brings communication to a halt quicker than the ranting and raving of an angry spouse.

On the other hand, some people have difficulty expressing their anger in any form. They close up like a clam while their rage boils within them. Some husbands and wives suppress this kind of anger and resentment for years. This is probably why the apostle Paul said, "Let not the sun go down upon your wrath" (Ephesians 4:26). If anger is dealt with on a daily basis, it will not have the opportunity to simmer inside and one day erupt into a violent explosion.

A story is told about a little girl who was walking down the street when a big dog came running toward her, barking ferociously. The girl froze, staring petrified at the big dog. Finally, a neighbor called to the dog, and the animal stopped barking. But the little girl remained standing very still. "It's all right, sweetie. The dog has stopped barking," the man said. The little girl did not reply. "It's all right now. The dog has stopped barking," he repeated. Finally, the little girl looked up and said, "Yes, but the bark is still on the inside."

Can you imagine the ferocious look on that dog's face? Has your spouse ever seen that expression on your face? Have you seen it in theirs? Is the communication in your marriage frozen by the fear of a violent outburst? Maybe your husband or wife has clammed up because the bark from your last argument is still ringing in his or her ears.

"Stop being mean, bad-tempered and angry. Quarreling, harsh words, and dislike of others should have no place in your lives" (Ephesians 4:31, *TLB*). Destructive anger is sin. Confess it as such, and let Jesus Christ cleanse this area of your life. Then pray for your spouse to be healed of any emotional damage your "barking" may have caused.

Opening The Lines Of Communication

If the level of communication in your marriage has broken down, Jay Adams has a suggestion that is guaranteed to generate interest. He says your spouse will always be delighted to discuss how *you* have wronged your husband or wife. If you can "confess your faults one to another, and pray one for another" (James 5:16), the lines of communication will be opened. Pride impedes honest sharing, but humility releases a flow of spontaneous give-and-take.

This week write a love letter to your spouse. Concentrate on one single topic: your mate's good points. What do you appreciate about your husband or wife? Put your thoughts down on paper. Focus only on the positive side of their character—not the negative aspects.

You will be amazed how this simple exercise will change your attitude. Then, as the way you perceive your mate is changed, the problems will begin to dissolve. In fact, many of them will disappear.

Communication is an art. We need to approach it the way we would learn to play the piano or the violin. Would you say, "Oh, I can't play the violin. I tried it once. In fact, I tried it several times, but it just didn't come naturally for me"? Some people give up trying to communicate with their spouse because they tried for a while and it didn't seem to work for them. Being a good communicator does not come naturally; it is a skill that must be learned and practiced.

If you are convinced that communication is the key to success in your marriage, then keep on trying. Persevere in working toward developing a relationship of intimate sharing with your husband or wife. The rewards will far outweigh any amount of effort you have to put forth. A rich, fulfilling experience awaits you.

"Be completely humble and gentle; be patient, bearing with one another in love. Make every effort to keep the unity of the Spirit through the bond of peace" (Ephesians 4:2-3, *NIV*). True unity develops as husband and wife share their lives by communicating with one another. Communication must, first of all, be intellectual, then emotional and spiritual—finally, it will be truly physical. The essence of marriage is *communication.*

Father, help us to tear down the barriers that prevent open and honest sharing in our marriage. Teach us to listen in love and speak the truth so we can raise the level of communication between us. May our words and attitudes reflect the love we have in our hearts for You and for our mate. In Jesus' name. Amen.

4

SAND IN YOUR SHOES?

Marriage can be either tremendously constructive or unimaginably destructive to the lives of those involved. Let's look at what makes the difference between a *constructive* and a *destructive* marriage.

Nothing is more beautiful than two people when they are first in love! Both think they have met the most wonderful person in the world. If family or friends try to candidly point out any faults in your beloved, their words are coldly received. Certainly nothing worthy of notice could begin to compare with the overwhelming good that flows from this dear one. Ah, the wonderful astigmatism of romance. Love, indeed, is blind!

When you fell in love with your husband or wife, did you have such feelings about your beloved? Did he or she share similar feelings with you? Were you lifted right up out of this world into the heavenlies? At last you had found someone who could look beyond the braces and the blemishes and see you for the wonderful person you really are; someone finally had true insight into your real character. This constructive aspect of love was remarkable because— wonder of wonders—you began to improve and become the person your beloved thought you to be.

Wouldn't it be wonderful if this potential for constructive betterment continued into married life? All too often, however, something else begins to occur. To your utter amazement, you soon discover your friends were right! He or she does have flaws. At first only the minutest ones are seen, and these can be overcome. But then things get worse—that big blob of toothpaste is *constantly* in the sink, the clothes are *always* left in the middle of the floor, and the door is *never* shut. As the little irritations begin to grow, it slowly dawns on you that, perhaps, you have been deceived—this person is *not* the man or woman you thought they were.

As you begin to concentrate on the negative aspects of your spouse's character, a shift in focus takes place. The lens is changed, and now the good points are all blurred. Instead, your husband or wife's glaring faults—the inconsiderateness, selfishness, and boorishness—all come into sharp focus.

Not only do you have this perception of your spouse, but you begin to convey to him or her how you feel. The principle that had worked to bring improvement when you were dating now works in a destructive way: your spouse begins to become whatever you say he or she is—an ill-mannered oaf, a lazy bum, a fat slob. And soon *what you say is what you get!*

Blinded By Criticism

Some years ago a man walked all the way from New York to California! At the end of his trek, reporters asked him if he had ever thought he wouldn't make it. "Many times," the man replied. When they asked what had almost defeated him, he answered, "Let me tell you. It wasn't the rushing traffic in the cities or the blaring horns and screeching brakes of cabs or trucks. It wasn't even those interminable mid-western plains that just went on and on as if they would never end. Nor was it the ice-tipped mountains of the Rockies or the blazing sun over the desert. What almost defeated me over and over again was *the sand in my shoes.*"

Although this unheralded, seldom-discussed irritant is never mentioned as the reason for divorce, "sand in the shoes" defeats many marriages. What is this irritating

36

problem that erodes away the very foundation of a harmonious marital relationship? It is the abrasive sand of *criticism*.

Criticism poisons the atmosphere of the home. Husbands and wives are afraid to say anything different or do anything special because a cutting word lies just beneath the surface, ready to lash out and cut them down. Marriage partners can no longer express love for their mate because of the rejection inherent in criticism. The bloom of love withers in an atmosphere of rejection, and divorce is often the result.

Faultfinding never accomplishes anything constructive. Criticism is sin because the faultfinder is trying to play God. Jesus said, "Do not judge, or you too will be judged. For in the same way you judge others, you will be judged, and with the measure you use, it will be measured to you" (Matthew 7:1-2, *NIV*).

In the physical world, for every action there is an equal and opposite reaction. Jesus tells us the same principle applies in the moral and spiritual realm. Yet, we blindly continue on with our degrading and destructive criticism, not realizing that we are only making our own lives more and more miserable.

The next time you open your lips to find fault with your husband or wife, remember that you are condemning yourself. Criticism is always *destructive*—to both the person being criticized and the one doing the criticizing. It lashes out at the victim but then recoils and strikes the criticizer in the back when he isn't looking.

Yes, ladies, you can get your husband to wipe his feet when he comes in the door. "I spent all day cleaning this room! Can't you ever remember to wipe your feet?" You can finally housebreak your husband and think you have gotten your point across. But in seventeen other ways you will receive your measure again, and you won't even know why or where it came from.

One day you will say, "How could he have done that to me! What did I do? Where did I go wrong? How could he even have looked at her? I've been such a faithful wife."

You've been faithful, all right—you have faithfully pointed out every fault in your husband for twenty-five years! He's had enough sand in his shoes.

"What can he possibly see in her? She's older than I am and not as pretty!" But she's probably a little smarter because she can't even see his faults! She actually thinks there are some really nice things about him—and she tells him frequently.

When you criticize your spouse, you blind his or her eyes to *your* good points. The more faults you point out, the more of your faults your mate will discover, until neither of you can see anything good in each other. You don't treat anyone else this way; you don't condemn your friends. Yet you make the greater mistake of derogating the one on whom most of your happiness in this life depends. And you reap the harvest of misery. After counseling with some couples, I have concluded they must be Mr. and Mrs. Frankenstein because both partners have painted a picture of some horrible monster.

All judgment proceeds from an attitude of pride; a proud person finds fault with others. Consider the Pharisee and the publican in the temple. The Pharisee said, "I thank thee, Lord, that I am not as other men." What an implicit criticism of the whole human race! "I don't do this; I don't do that. I'm not like that publican over there at the other end of the temple." The publican, however, would not so much as lift up his eyes to heaven but smote his breast and cried, "God, be merciful to me a sinner." This man wasn't looking around finding fault with other people; he had a spirit of humility, and all he could see was his own sin. (See Luke 18:9-14.)

This is what Jesus meant when He asked, "Why do you look at the speck of sawdust in your brother's eye and pay no attention to the plank in your own eye?" (Matthew 7:3, *NIV*). The plank in your eye is this unhealthy attitude of *pride* that judges and finds fault with others.

You say to your spouse, "Here, let me take that speck out of your eye," when a two-by-four beam is sticking out of your own. One has to be totally blind to the beam in his own eye before he can focus on the speck in another's eye. When a person comes under the conviction of the Holy Spirit, sees the sin in his own life, and says, "Woe is me, I am an unclean," he is not as likely to see the fault in his spouse's eye.

Goodfinding Vs. Faultfinding

Some of you are saying, "You mean I am never supposed to say anything critical about my husband or wife?" The Bible deals with that too. We are told, "If a man be overtaken in a fault, ye which are spiritual, restore such an one in the spirit of meekness; considering thyself lest thou also be tempted" (Galatians 6:1). Notice: it is a brother *overtaken* in a fault; it is not nit-picking at every little thing. That is the law of the jungle, where an animal is singled out by its predator and then later devoured by scavengers that pick and claw at its remains.

Some people suppose themselves to be spiritual because they can see the faults in others. They do not realize they are not acting like God; they are acting like the beasts of the jungle. God, in His infinite love, covers a multitude of sins. He looked down upon us in all our uncleanness, with all our faults, and sent His dearly beloved Son to die for us. God's way is the way of love, and love covers a multitude of sins. (See 1 Peter 4:8, *NIV*).

Instead of pointing out our faults to us, Jesus took them upon Himself on the cross, bearing the burden of our guilt and the penalty for our sins. Christ is the *friend* of sinners—not the faultfinder of sinners. If we ask Him to forgive us of our sin, trusting in Him for salvation, Jesus accepts us as righteous. Acceptance—that is the purpose of redemption.

How can we who have been forgiven and accepted by a loving Savior turn around, criticize, and reject our spouse?

If we want to love the way Jesus loves, we must strive to accept our husband or wife and overlook their faults.

How can you get rid of the sand of criticism in your marriage? How can you make the principle of *what you say is what you get* work in a constructive way? First of all, get rid of all resentment by forgiving your mate and asking them to forgive you for your sin of pride and criticism.

The next step is to determine you will try to find the good points in your mate. God's Word tells us how to do this: "Whatever is true, whatever is noble, whatever is right, whatever is pure, whatever is lovely, whatever is admirable—if anything is excellent or praiseworthy—think about such things" (Philippians 4:8, *NIV*).

Think about the good things your spouse does. Take time to meditate on the positive aspects of your mate's character, and pray that God will give you eyes to see only good. Creatively consider what is good about your spouse. Pray about what caused you to marry your beloved. Every day share with your spouse something good. Instead of the same hackneyed, trite points you have managed to say before, express something new you have discovered about them.

The book of Proverbs tells us, "Withhold not good from them to whom it is due, when it is in the power of thine hand to do it" (3:27). The only way your husband or wife can know how you feel is for you to send clear and unambiguous signals that express your love. Don't withhold verbal expressions of your love; tell your spouse exactly how you feel about him or her. Everybody needs to know they have top priority in someone's affections.

A happy husband once said to his wife, "You reached into my life and found the good no one else had ever seen." A marriage can be destructive or constructive. Whether you see and share the faults or see and share the virtues is the determining factor. You can expect tremendous positive results when you begin to practice goodfinding instead of faultfinding.

One of the most practical formulas for strengthening husband/wife relationships was developed by Dr. Ed Wheat, a marriage counselor, physician, speaker, and author. In his book, *Love Life For Every Married Couple,* Dr. Wheat uses the acronym B-E-S-T to describe his method of improving the marital relationship: Blessing, Edifying, Sharing, Touching. We will deal with the importance of sharing and touching in later chapters, but the first two parts of this formula offer the antidote to faultfinding and criticism.

In the acrostic BEST, the "B" stands for *blessing.* In the New Testament, the word "blessing" comes from the Greek word *eulogia,* which simply means to "speak well of." Blessing our spouse means to speak well of him or her. It is the opposite of criticizing, nagging, or faultfinding.

First of all, blessing means that we will speak kindly *to* our husband or wife. We are to compliment them and encourage them with our words. Encouragement and compliments tend to motivate people, stimulating them to do better. Criticism and faultfinding, however, are a depressant and tend to cause people to do less. By speaking well *to* our spouse, we can motivate them to improve in the areas where they are weak.

Secondly, we need to speak well *about* them. I am sometimes astonished by what husbands and wives say *to* one another and *about* one another in public. Some couples think snide remarks are clever or funny, but they pay the price for their comments in the privacy of their own home. How well do you speak of your spouse in front of other people?

Thirdly, we need to express appreciation and thankfulness for what our spouse *does.* Unfortunately, this sometimes degenerates into a few simple things for which we are grateful. Some husbands view marriage as a kind of business arrangement. "I make the living. You keep the house and the kids. That's the deal. I do my part; you do yours. Who's to thank for what?'' That attitude might make a good working arrangement, but it makes a lousy marriage. We need to be creative in showing appreciation and thankfulness rather than simply applauding the same things over and over again.

Fourthly, we need to pray regularly God's blessings *upon* our spouse. We will pray for famine-stricken Ethiopia and the missionaries around the world yet fail to pray regularly for God's blessing upon our spouse. Oh, yes, we pray for their health; we pray for their business success; we pray for their safety. But do we really pray God's richest blessing upon their innermost being? We should pray that they would become all God would have them to be and that they would experience the fullness of joy God wants them to enjoy.

The "E" in Dr. Wheat's acrostic BEST is for *edifying*. Derived from the word *edifice,* it simply means "to build up." Instead of tearing each other down, we should be building one another up. We need to undergird our spouse and support them. You can help develop your husband or wife's self-image by building his or her confidence and encouraging your mate to become a well-balanced person. We often do this for our children but fail to realize that our spouse has the same needs. Everyone has feelings of inadequacy, inferiority, weakness, and inability. When these are minimized by a spouse who emphasizes our strengths and talents, our self-esteem grows and makes it possible for us to do even greater things.

In Louis H. Evans' book, *Your Marriage: Duel or Duet?,* I found this poem by an unknown author. It describes perfectly how this principle of minimizing the bad and emphasizing the good works.

> I love you,
> Not only for what you are,
> But for what I am
> When I am with you.

I love you,
Not only for what
You have made of yourself,
But for what
You are making of me.

I love you,
For the part of me
That you bring out;
I love you
For putting your hand
Into my heaped-up heart
And passing over
All the foolish, weak things
That you can't help
Dimly seeing there,
And for drawing out
Into the light
All the beautiful belongings
That no one else had looked
Quite far enough to find.

I love you because you
Are helping me to make
Of the lumber of my life
Not a tavern
But a temple;
Out of the works
Of my every day
Not a reproach
But a song. . . .

I love you.

Begin today to shake the sand out of your marital shoes.
Let the words of your mouth and the meditation of your

heart be acceptable in God's sight. Then what you say will get you the kind of marriage you want.

Father, may we be a constructive force in the life of our spouse. Help us to be an encourager, an uplifter, and a goodfinder. Help us to know what it means to be truly spiritual and to be filled with love that covers a multitude of sins. For Jesus' sake, who thus loved us and clothed us with His righteousness. Amen.

5
MAKING MARRIAGE WORK

Have you ever bought a new appliance but couldn't figure out how to make it work? That's when you need to heed the advice of a poster I once saw, "When all else fails, read the instructions."

In America today, the institution of marriage is in serious trouble. In some states we now have each year an equal or larger number of divorces than marriages. In fact, Americans have achieved the worst record of marital failure in the history of mankind! What a tragic indictment.

You would suppose that any group of people who had experienced such obvious failure would be anxious to consult the Maker, read the instructions, ascertain the problem, and discover how to make marriage work. Yet that is not the case. Americans add one idiotic alteration after another to the mechanism of marriage—living together, open marriages, marriage contracts, communes. Then, when those twists in the machinery don't work, someone suggests abandoning marriage as an institution altogether.

America's approach to marital problems reminds me of an alcoholic whose drinking has brought him to the place where his boss has fired him, his money is all gone, his wife has left him, his home has been reclaimed, and his children hate him. At last, he decides to do something about the problem, so—he reaches for the bottle! "How stupid," you say. Yet many people think the answer to their marital problems is reaching for the divorce papers.

The Manufacturer's Instructions

Marriage for many couples becomes a battlefield that transforms their home into a literal hell on earth. David Engelsma, in his book, *Marriage: The Mystery of Christ and the Church,* puts it this way:

> In the world, marriage is the battlefield on which a vicious, relentless struggle rages between the tyrant-husband and the rebel-wife. Now the one, now the other is temporarily victorious. At present, in our society, the rebellious woman has the upper hand. If the world lasts, the male will again assert himself, overthrow the woman's dominance, and rule her more tyrannically than before. The Christian marriage is radically different. The husband rules in love. The wife submits in love. Marriage, thus, is not a framework for bitterest strife and mutual destruction, but a relationship of fellowship, joy, and mutual help. There is peace.

The Biblical solution to the problem is to take the tyrant out of the husband and the rebel out of the wife. Peace! That is God's answer.

To reject God's solution is analagous to a tattered, dirty beggar from skid row questioning Rockefeller's principles of banking and economics. That would be ludicrous. For us, who have proved such miserable failures in the area of marriage, to question God's formula for a peaceful home is more tragic than ludicrous.

Suppose we do decide to go back to the Manufacturer's instructions on how to make a marriage work. Where do we find them? The fifth chapter of Ephesians contains some very interesting and controversial guidelines for the marriage relationship. Yet, as we read them, let us remember they are *commands* from God's Word.

"Wives, *submit* yourselves unto your own husbands, as unto the Lord. For the husband is the head of the wife, even as Christ is the head of the church: and he is the saviour of the body. Therefore as the church is *subject* unto Christ, so let the wives be to their own husbands in every thing. Husbands, *love* your wives, even as Christ also loved the church, and gave himself for it"— Ephesians 5:22-25, italics added.

A certain anxiety came over me as I faced this passage. I wished—for fear of being called a male chauvinist—that the apostle Paul had started with the instructions to the husband instead of the wife. To my surprise, I discovered I was not the only minister who shunned this topic. When I consulted Spurgeon, I found he skipped all the instructions given to the wife in this passage and dealt only with the husband. Criswell, in his excellent commentary on Ephesians, omitted this portion of chapter five altogether.

The apostle Paul, however, jumped right in without flinching. So I thought, Well, Kennedy, you've never backed away from a challenge before, and you're not going to run from this one. You are going to deal with this subject head on. And so I am!

Art Linkletter once read an interesting letter a little girl had written to God. "Dear God," she wrote, "are boys better than girls? I know that you are one, but try to be fair." Right from the beginning, let's understand that God is neither a boy nor a man. All concepts of human sexuality break down when we consider the infinite Spirit who is God. In the gospel accounts, Jesus' treatment of women and His sensitivity to their needs portray the heart of God. Our heavenly Father has no favorites.

You may agree with that point, but then ask, "What about the apostle Paul? Everyone knows he didn't like women."

After preaching in a church in New York City, I got into a discussion about the apostle Paul with a young "liberated" woman. She could not understand how such a prejudiced man ever managed to get his writings included as part of holy Scripture. This revealed a great deal to me about her whole view of Christianity, the Bible, the inspiration and revelation of God, and the authority of God Himself as it is revealed in His Word.

If you believe that the scriptures are the revelation of God, then you must accept the writings of Paul as inspired by the Holy Spirit. John Calvin said that we are to receive the words of Scripture as if they dripped from the lips of God. Remember, these are not my opinions but clear declarations from the Word of God. If you disagree, you are not disagreeing with me or the apostle Paul; you are disagreeing with God, and your argument is not with me but with Him.

Take Me To Your Leader

Two people riding a horse cannot both steer the same animal; someone must be the guide. You cannot go two ways at once. Two generals cannot supervise the same army; nor can two presidents manage the same bank. Only one person can be in authority. God's Word has a great deal to say about authorities and submission to them. A king's subjects must respect his authority; servants must be in subjection to their masters; children are to obey their parents; and wives are to submit to their husbands.

As I considered the various scriptural texts dealing with the wife's relationship to her husband, one central theme emerged. It is found not only in the passage from Ephesians but frequently throughout the New Testament. See if you can discern what it is.

> Wives, *submit* yourselves unto your own husbands—Ephesians 5:22.
> As the church is *subject* unto Christ, so let the wives be to their own husbands in every thing—Ephesians 5:24.

> Let . . . the wife see that she *reverence* her husband—Ephesians 5:33.
>
> Wives, *submit* yourselves unto your own husbands, as it is fit in the Lord—Colossians 3:18.
>
> Wives, *be in subjection* to your own husbands—1 Peter 3:1.
>
> The holy women also, who trusted in God . . . *being in subjection* unto their own husbands. Even as Sara *obeyed* Abraham, calling him lord—1 Peter 3:5.
>
> The *head* of the woman is the man—1 Corinthians 11:3.

What is the central theme of God's Word concerning the wife's relationship to her husband? *Submission.* The wife is commanded to be in submission to her husband. For some women that is a hard pill to swallow.

In this day and age, no one wants to be in submission to anyone. Rebellion is the order of the times; submission is out, and rebellion is in. The generation gap is simply children throwing off the authority of their parents. The feminist movement is the rebellion of wives against their husbands and other men in authority. "No man is going to tell me what to do!" One of the reasons for the widespread rebellion of children against parents stems from the rebellion of wives against the authority of their husbands.

While some reject the whole idea of submission, others try to redefine the teachings of Scripture and strive to make it mean something else. But the Greek verb *hupotasso* means "to submit" or "to be in subjection"; and the meaning is the same throughout the New Testament.

You might ask, "Why should the woman be in subjection? Why shouldn't the man submit to the woman and be in subjection to her?" In some homes, that's the way it is.

Suppose one Saturday a spaceship from Mars were to land in your backyard, and a little green creature were to crawl out. What would happen if he went over to your children

49

and said, "Take me to your leader"? Where would they take him? Whom do your children consider the head of your house?

Who Made You Boss?

Have you ever been asked, "Who's the boss around here anyway?" Whether it is you or someone else, one thing is for sure—someone has to be the boss. Our heavenly Father had some very good reasons for making the *man,* and not the woman, the boss. Let's look at why God placed the husband as head of the family.

The most basic reason for the husband's authority is that God created man before woman and placed him in a state of preeminence in the Garden of Eden. "The head of every man is Christ; and the head of the woman is the man . . . forasmuch as he is the image and glory of God: but the woman is the glory of the man" (1 Corinthians 11:3,7). Why is a woman not to usurp man's authority over her? Because "Adam was first formed, then Eve" (1 Timothy 2:12-13).

The feminist's opinion is that God created man, took one look at him, and said, "Oh, I can do better than that;" so He made woman. This kind of rebellious attitude views God as some sort of bungler who knows nothing about the husband/wife relationship and didn't know how to make people in the first place.

God had a specific purpose in mind when He created woman. "The Lord God said, 'It is not good for the man to be alone. I will make a helper suitable for him' " (Genesis 2:18, *NIV*). The wife was not created to serve her own self interests; she was created *for* her husband. "Neither was the man created for the woman; but the woman for the man" (1 Corinthians 11:9).

Modern women reject this fundamental virtue of the wife, claiming that she is an equal partner in marriage. They insist that marriage is a contract where no one is the final authority in the relationship—every decision is made by mutual agreement. The wife considers herself independent of her husband—with her own life, her own career, her own fulfillment as a woman apart from her husband. Her main goal in life is not to be a helper for her husband but to satisfy her own desires and achieve her own success. Such thinking is rebellion against the divine creation order of God.

In fact, this is exactly where Eve went wrong. God placed man as head of the marriage relationship because the woman had trouble following orders. "Adam was not the one deceived; it was the woman who was deceived and became a sinner" (1 Timothy 2:14, *NIV*). Because the woman was the first to sin, God told her, "Your desire will be for your husband, and he will rule over you" (Genesis 3:16, *NIV*).

Rebellion is still Satan's most effective temptation. It worked on Eve in the garden, so he continues to use it on women today. Satan himself is the arch rebel who refused to be a creature subservient to God. When he rebelled against the divine creation order of God, the world was plunged into sin and chaos. A wife who rebels against God's order for the marriage relationship will throw her home and family into confusion and disorder. Woman's fallen nature is basically a rebel nature that must first be changed by the regenerating work of the Holy Spirit before she can even begin to submit to her husband.

How do wives rebel against the creation order God has established for the home? Some rebel openly, refusing to submit to their husbands in any way. Others ignore their husbands, go their own way, and live independent lives. They sleep in the same house, eat at the same table, but do their own thing. By refusing to be the helper to their husband that God created them to be, they are in rebellion against their Creator.

Some wives obey outwardly, but inwardly they are filled with bitterness and rebellion. They partially assent to submission by yielding themselves to meet the material and physical needs of their husbands. Like a maid or a servant, they take care of the home, the meals, and the children; but when it comes to inwardly yielding to being their husbands' helpmeet, they rebel.

Submission is an inward attitude of heart that leads to obedience. Your adornment "should be that of your inner self, the unfading beauty of a gentle and quiet spirit, which is of great worth in God's sight. For this is the way the holy women of the past who put their hope in God used to make themselves beautiful. They were submissive to their own husbands" (1 Peter 3:4-6, *NIV*).

How Far Is Too Far?

Whenever headship in the husband/wife relationship is discussed, the question most often asked is, "Are there any limits to a wife's submission?" My answer to that question is based on the biblical concept of authority.

First of all, God's Word teaches that all authority is from God. No human being in and of himself has any authority at all. The only authority man has comes from God. The Bible also teaches that all human authority is limited to its proper sphere; no human authority has unlimited power. A parent has authority over his children, but he does not have the right to abuse them. No human authority can countermand the direct authority of God. A sergeant cannot override the orders of the general; the pupil cannot contradict the rules set down by the teacher. If any human authority endeavors to contradict God's commands, the Christian is bound by conscience to obey God rather than man.

What about an unbelieving husband? Is the wife to submit herself to him? Yes, unless the husband expects her to do something specifically forbidden by God; or if he forbids her to do something that God specifically commands her to do. When that happens, she should graciously, and in submission, do what God has said in His Word.

Submission is an attitude of the heart—whether the wife agrees with her husband or not. "Wives, in the same way be submissive to your husbands so that, if any of them do not believe the word, they may be won over without talk by the behavior of their wives, when they see the purity and reverence of your lives" (1 Peter 3:1-2, *NIV*).

I read about a minister and his wife who enjoyed a beautiful relationship. A young seminarian had observed this couple on several occasions and noticed that the husband would do anything for his wife. The young man wondered about this until he came to live with their family while he attended seminary. Every afternoon, the wife disappeared for a while. Later, she emerged from her bedroom wearing a fresh dress, having her hair styled, and smelling of perfume—just in time to meet her husband at the door with a big hug and kiss. The young seminary student thought how wise this wife was. Her simple act of submission showed a deep respect and admiration for her husband that he reciprocated in many ways. This helped create the beautiful relationship they enjoyed together.

A wife who has a submissive heart will seek to please her husband because she loves and respects him. Her reward will be a devoted, affectionate spouse who will go out of his way to provide, protect, and care for her. Who could ask for anything more?

Heavenly Father, we want our homes to come under the rules of authority that You have established in Your Word. Help us, as husbands and wives, to submit to You and to one another in a way that is pleasing to You and in obedience to Your commands. In Jesus' name. Amen.

6

MISTAKES HUSBANDS OFTEN MAKE

After hearing a sermon on the husband/wife relationship, a couple told me what their little boy said as they were going to the car: "Gee, Dad, you've got the easy part. Mom has to submit to you, and all you have to do is love her."

It might seem that the Bible places the husband on a high pedestal of imperious sovereignty from which he looks down on his wife in her place of submission. But let's look at what God's Word actually says about this matter:

> "Husbands, *love* your wives, even as Christ also loved the church, and gave himself for it. . . . So ought men to *love* their wives as their own bodies. He that *loveth* his wife loveth himself. For no man ever yet hated his own flesh; but nourisheth and cherisheth it, even as the Lord the church. . . . Nevertheless let every one of you in particular so *love* his wife even as himself" (Ephesians 5:25-33).

That is quite a challenge—to love your wife the way Christ loves the church; to give of yourself to your wife the way Jesus gave Himself for us. Not an easy assignment—for even the bravest among us. Nothing less than absolute commitment and determination will enable any man to obey this command. In fact, without the power of the Holy Spirit, it is humanly impossible.

Problems occur when a husband reads this passage about his position of headship and starts thinking he is to exercise some form of harsh tyranny over his spouse. Having discovered that she is subject to him, he concludes that his will is sovereign and what he says goes! He begins to strut around the house like a little Caesar or Napoleon, ruling with despotic control over his family. Yet the apostle Paul says nothing about the husband *controlling* the wife; the command is to *love* her.

Some husbands abuse their position because they do not read *how* they are to be the head—as Christ is the head of the Church and the Savior of the body. Jesus Christ has infinite power and all authority, yet He lovingly leads us, not by pushing and shoving but by showing us a more excellent way. Wisdom and restraint are the keys to loving, effective leadership. A husband who keeps his eyes on Jesus and acts according to His character will be blessed with a loyal, devoted wife who respects and admires him.

The purpose of headship is to keep the body out of trouble. As part of our human body, the head keeps the hand from burning itself and the foot from stepping on a nail. The command is to love your wife the way you love your own body—as much as you love yourself. Husbands, you are the head of your marriage relationship, and it is your responsibility to protect and care for your wife.

Some women nag their husbands and try to make them more loving. "If you loved me, you would do this and wouldn't do that." This kind of feminine manipulation is as much out of line as the husband who tries to terrorize his wife into submission.

Many husbands make the mistake of thinking they must *make* their wives submit to them. But God's Word contains no such instruction. The wife must voluntarily submit, just as the Church voluntarily submits to the Lord. If your wife does not submit to you, that is not your problem—it is hers. She must answer to God for her rebellion.

While the wife is under the authority of the husband, the husband is also under authority. He must look to Jesus and seek God's will and direction for his family. When Christ is sovereign in a home, love reigns supreme.

Persons And Things

Have you ever thought about what the word *husband* really means? It comes from the words "house-band"; the husband is a band that reaches around his house to protect it, hold it up, provide for it, and defend it from outside dangers.

One of the husband's main responsibilities is to provide for the financial and economic well-being of his household. For this reason, God created man with a physical and emotional makeup that enables him to go out and compete in the workplace. Unfortunately, in today's society, many men are failing in this basic responsibility, and more and more wives have to go out and get a job. Some women must work, but other women work because the husband is failing in his God-ordained duty to provide for his family.

When a mother has to work outside the home, the effect on the children—and the husband—can be devastating. Our society is already reaping the results of children who come home from school every day to an empty house. One of the main causes of delinquency among young people is the lack of stability and security that results when both parents work. A husband who forces his wife to work so they can have all the "extras" is actually robbing himself and his children of the "necessities."

At the opposite end of the spectrum are husbands who suppose that by providing things for their wives and children they have fulfilled their obligation to love their family. A man who thinks this way may awake one morning to find that his wife is miserable and his children don't respect him. With righteous indignation, he cries, "What did I do to deserve this kind of treatment? Didn't I give them everything they wanted?'' Yes, you did, but you failed to give them what they needed most: a personal relationship with you as husband and father.

One of the greatest causes of marital failure is the confusion over the difference between persons and things. We have trouble understanding that we are to *love* people and *use* things. In fact, things should be used to help us develop our relationships with those we love. Unfortunately, most of the people in this world love *things* and use *people* to get what they want.

Balance comes when we learn to put people before things and use things to help meet the needs of those we love. Husbands who have their priorities in order will work hard to provide for their wife and children without becoming workaholics who neglect their family relationships.

Women fall into this same trap. Because of the nesting instinct, their concern for the house, and their responsibility to care for the children, they often fail to recognize what is most important—the people living in the home. Wives, do you want to know whether or not you put things before people? Then answer this question: Your husband walks in the door and leaves muddy footprints all over the just-waxed floor. How do you react? What is foremost in your mind? Your relationship with your husband or the kitchen floor? Wives who become fixated with things may one day find themselves left with a neatly cared-for, but empty, house.

Whom Do You Love?

Earlier, we discussed the independent wife who refuses to be a helper to her husband and seeks her own fulfillment apart from her mate. You husbands would be the first to say that she is out of God's divine order. But what about the husband who has his fishing buddies, his sports activities, and his hobbies and interests without giving any thought to his wife's needs? You know her—the golfer's lonely wife or the football widow.

I heard about a wife who had reached the limit of her frustration level near the end of football season. Her husband had been glued to the television every Saturday and Sunday, completely ignoring his wife. One weekend she had had enough. She planted herself in front of the television, stomped her foot, and said, "Now, I want to know, which do you love more, me or football?" After a long period of silence, her husband finally looked up at her, smiled feebly, and replied, "I love you more than hockey."

Although few men would admit they love football more than their wives, their actions display an independent lifestyle that says, "I don't need you." And that hurts.

Some husbands refer to Scripture for their defense. "But wasn't man created to be an independent creature? Wasn't the wife made as a helpmeet for him?" Yes, the woman was made for man, but God gave her to him because man needed help! Man was not sufficient himself; he needed someone to help him and share his life. In fact, God said it wasn't good for man to be alone; independence was never part of the Creator's original purpose for marriage partners. The husband who lives his own life, stopping now and then at home to refuel is defying God and declaring that it *is* good for man to be alone.

Ignoring your wife while you pursue your own pleasures shows a lack of respect for her. God's Word makes it very clear how a husband is to treat his wife. "Husbands, in the same way be considerate as you live with your wives, and treat them with respect as the weaker partner and as heirs with you of the gracious gift of life, so that nothing will hinder your prayers" (1 Peter 3:7, *NIV*).

How you treat your wife is a test of your Christian faith and your love for God. "If anyone says, 'I love God,' yet hates his brother, he is a liar. For anyone who does not love his brother, whom he has seen, cannot love God, whom he has not seen. And he has given us this command: Whoever loves God must also love his brother" (1 John 4:20-21, *NIV*).

We learned in an earlier chapter that love is *doing* and *enduring*. You show your wife that you love her by being polite, considerate, and attentive to her.

Making Or Breaking Her Day

When you were engaged, you gave a lot of thought to how you could make your fiancee happy. You put a lot of creative energy into making her day with special treats and surprises. But now that you are married, other priorities have taken over—you have to go to work; you have your business to run; you have a home and cars to take care of; you have to provide for your family.

Making your spouse's day is about 296th on your priority list—especially at seven o'clock in the morning. But the way you and your wife part from each other in the morning can make or break the day. Your leave-taking paints the hues on the background of both her mind and yours, predetermining the attitude with which you will return home in the evening. How do you exit from the house in the morning? This poem by Dr. Louis Evans sums up the importance of making leaving a positive experience.

> If I had known in the morning
> How wearily all the day
> The word unkind
> Would trouble my mind
> I said when you [or I] went away,
> I had been more careful, darling,
> Nor given you needless pain;
> But we vex our own
> With look and tone
> We might never take back again.
>
> For though in the quiet evening
> You may give me the kiss of peace,
> Yet it might be

That never for me
The pain of the heart should cease.
How many go forth in the morning
That never come home at night,
And hearts have broken
For harsh words spoken
That sorrow can ne'er set right.

We have careful thoughts for the stranger
And smiles for the sometime guest.
But oft our own
The bitter tone,
Though we love our own the best.
Oh, lips with the curve impatient,
And bow with that look of scorn,
'Twere a cruel fate
Were the night too late
To undo the work of the morn.

Don't make the mistake of leaving your precious wife with cruel and unkind words ringing in her ears all day long. You never know when those may be the last words she ever hears you say.

Husbands make many mistakes, but most can be easily corrected by simply being more considerate and sensitive to your wife's needs. You'd be surprised to find how little it takes to make her happy. Most men have a tendency to overlook the obvious, so try asking your wife for specific ways you can please her. It could change your marriage!

Most of all, don't forget that as you put the Manufacturer's instructions to work in your marriage, it will become a smooth-running machine. When the tyrant-husband has been changed by Christ and replaced by a loving one and the rebel-wife has been tamed by the Holy Spirit and given a submissive heart, joy and peace will fill your marriage and home.

Heavenly Father, by the power of Your sword-like Word in the hands of the Holy Spirit, change the tyrant-husbands and tame the rebel-wives. In their place raise up loving husbands and submissive wives who will love and respect one another. To the glory of Jesus Christ. Amen.

7

WHEN YOU'RE GOING IN DIFFERENT DIRECTIONS

While waiting in the Chicago train station, a young man was thrilled to meet and chat with a lovely young lady. A delight to behold and a pleasure to talk with, she captivated his attention. When the call for the train came over the loudspeaker, she stood. He immediately jumped up and said, "May I sit next to you on the train?"

She replied, "I'm sorry, but you can't."

Somewhat confused and feeling dejected, he asked, "Oh, you're traveling with someone?"

"No."

"Then why can't I sit next to you?"

She answered, "Because you're going to New York, and I'm going to California!"

It is difficult, if not impossible, for two people to develop a meaningful relationship when they're going in different directions. Our heavenly Father knew this, and He gave us these instructions through the apostle Paul:

> Do not be unequally yoked together with unbelievers. For what do righteousness and wickedness have in common? Or what fellowship can light have with darkness? What harmony is there between Christ and Belial? What does a believer have in common with an unbeliever? What agreement is there between the temple of God and idols?—2 Corinthians 6:14-16, *NIV*.

A Christian man or woman should marry only another believer—not someone who merely claims to be a nominal Christian but a genuine born-again believer who truly trusts in Christ as Savior. Those who disregard the injunctions of God's Word are disobeying His commands and will undoubtedly reap the pain and heartbreak that spiritual incompatability in marriage always brings.

Sometimes spiritual incompatability occurs after a couple is married—when one partner becomes a believer. Then we have the situation of a Christian living with a non-Christian. What is to be done? Sometimes the Christian will say, "Well, I should leave this man or woman because he or she is not a believer. I'm a Christian, committed to Christ, and I shouldn't live in this ungodly atmosphere."

The apostle Paul says no. If the unbelieving partner is willing to remain in the marriage, then the believer should not be the one to leave. "How do you know, wife, whether you will save your husband? Or, how do you know, husband, whether you will save your wife?" (1 Corinthians 7:16, *NIV*).

Cracking The Nut

If the Christian is not to leave, what should he or she do? The believing husband is to follow all the Bible's commands regarding loving his wife and treating her with consideration. (See 1 Peter 3:7.) That is enough to bring most women to the Lord.

On the other hand, a believing wife needs more specific directions on how to win her unbelieving husband. The *King James Version* says the husbands will be won "by the conversation of their wives." Three hundred years ago when this version of the Bible was translated, the word "conversation" meant your manner of life and had nothing to do with speaking. Unfortunately, many wives take this instruction at face value and do just the opposite of what the Bible says. A more modern version puts it this way: "Wives . . . be submissive to your husbands so that if any of them do not believe the word, they may be won over *without talk* by the behavior of their wives, when they see the purity and reverence of your lives" (1 Peter 3:1-2, *NIV*, italics added).

Sometimes a wife preaches at her unconverted husband night and day with one sermon after another. Then she complains, "My husband won't ever go to church!" No wonder. He hears it all day long from his own, personal unordained female preacher who's got three points and a moral to go with anything she does!

Dr. C. S. Lovett has an interesting word of advice for anyone married to an unbeliever. In his book, *Unequally Yoked Wives,* he describes the "nutcracker technique." We are all familiar with a nutcracker. When a nut is placed between the handles and the pressure is applied, the nut is cracked. Dr. Lovett compares the two handles of the nutcracker to our *works* and our *light.* Jesus said, "Let your light so shine before men, that they may see your good works, and glorify your Father which is in heaven" (Matthew 5:16).

Dr. Lovett describes the woman who goes to church five times a week, reads her Bible every day, prays for hours, and puts Christ above everything else—particularly above her husband to whom she is continually preaching. Her "light" looks and sounds more like fireworks. The submission and respect the Bible talks about is missing from her relationship with her husband.

Other Christian husbands and wives live godly lives, but they never tell their mate or anyone else why they are doing the things that they are doing. Consequently, they have works but no light. Their works are wasted because they do not praise their Father in heaven. The light isn't set forth to show that Christ is the source of the joy and peace in their lives. In order to be an effective witness in the home, good deeds must be accompanied by an acknowledgement of the reason for the "hope that is in you" (1 Peter 3:15).

The ideal is to have the *works*—the joyous, glad submission of the wife to her husband; or the considerate love of a believing husband for his wife—combined with the *light*. Let's see how this can be put into practice in a marriage.

A woman married to an unbeliever says, "My husband's always complaining because he can't stand instant coffee for breakfast. But I'm not going to get up in the middle of the night to perk coffee when instant tastes just as good!" But what would happen if she did?

The next morning when her husband walks into the kitchen, he notices something different: the aroma of fresh-perked coffee! He looks down in amazement to find his coffee cup filled and waiting for him. The wife has done a good *work*.

Her husband says, "Hey, what's this? Fresh-perked coffee?"

Now the *light*: His wife said, "You know, dear, I've been praying about our relationship as husband and wife. I know the Lord wants me to be a good wife to you. He wants me to please you, and I want to obey God's Word. I thought this was something you would enjoy, so from now on you will be having fresh-perked coffee."

The husband is squeezed between the wife's work and her light. Her husband is delighted, and Christ is glorified. Those of you with unbelieving spouses should try the "nutcracker technique." You might be amazed at the results.

How's Your Compatibility?

Someone gave me this definition of *incompatibility*: the husband provides the income, and the wife provides the patibility. Wouldn't it be wonderful if it were that easy? We all know that achieving compatibility between marriage partners requires effort and constant growth by both husband and wife. In addition to spiritual incompatibility, there are other areas where a husband and wife may not be in agreement.

66

One place where many couples experience incompatibility is in the bedroom. A judge who had heard divorce cases for over thirty years said that the underlying reason for the overwhelming majority of divorces was sexual incompatibility.

Millions of American women are experiencing little if any sexual satisfaction in their marriage. A female doctor said clinical studies show that from 40 to 50 percent of American women have some form of the *hypoaesthetic syndrome*, commonly called *frigidity*. Many wives are suffering from total sexual anesthesia: complete and total absence of any sexual feelings at all.

If you could sit behind a pastoral counseling desk and hear the anguish of husbands and wives trying to deal with this problem, you would know how serious it is. You would hear men say that they wake up in the night, look at their wives, and despise them. You would hear the sobs of brokenhearted women whose marriages have turned into an arid wasteland or a horrible nightmare.

Many people hold completely erroneous ideas concerning this matter of sexual relations and adjustment in marriage. One of the basic causes of frigidity results from the American woman's concept of the marital relationship and her role as a wife. She is barraged on every side by conflicting input regarding her identity as a woman and her need for fulfillment.

Modern society has confused the issue and forced women to find their identity outside the home. Their fulfillment no longer comes from being a homemaker and housewife, thus making wives feel insignificant and unnecessary. To fill the void, today's woman seeks status and equality with men in the working world.

The feminist movement tells her, "You've come a long way, baby. Assert yourself and enter into man's arena. You can compete with them because you are the superior sex." Many women have followed this advice and become the dominant personality in the marriage. In many cases, the wife has taken over as head of the home, having assumed the position of decision-maker and breadwinner. A woman who enters into competitiveness with her husband begins to view him as a threat. When this happens, the wife cannot respond to him sexually.

Clinical studies show that a female child reared in the home of a dominant, masculine mother will, because of the attitudes toward men instilled in her mind and heart, be rendered frigid by the age of five. Many girls are taught that males are basically the enemy who seek to subjugate and dominate females. For this reason men must be competed with and regarded as animalistic beasts who take advantage of women for their own lustful pleasure. No wonder so many women today grow up with feelings of rejection, anger, guilt, and envy toward their brothers, fathers, and spouses. This attitude has produced in many women a complete inability to ever fully enter into their God-given birthright: the fulfillment of womanhood in the holy bonds of matrimony.

Sex—An Original Idea

In the past, women were taught that sexual desire was a male propensity and respectable women shouldn't exhibit any need for it. The church has helped foster this teaching with legalistic dogma and man-made rules. Many women today suppose that sexuality is really a male characteristic—at least more so than a female characteristic.

In the last thirty years, an overwhelming amount of scientific study has been done in the area of sexuality. One incontestable proof has been brought to light: A woman in her normal state has as much sexual desire as any man.

This recent discovery by scientists and psychologists comes as no surprise to the One who created male and female. In the very first chapter of the Bible, we read that God made two sexes, not one: "Male and female he created them. . . . God saw all that he had made, and it was very good" (Genesis 1:27,31, *NIV*). The maleness of the man and the femaleness of the woman are good in God's sight.

God created sex. Some people have the idea that God made men and women, and the devil came along later and pinned sex on them. Yet the very first thing God told people to do was to have sex—that was the first verbal commandment given to mankind. "God blessed them and said to them, 'Be fruitful and increase in number' " (Genesis 1:28, *NIV*). God is in favor of sex.

This principle is reinforced in the New Testament by the apostle Paul:

> The husband should fulfill his marital duty to his wife, and likewise the wife to her husband. The wife's body does not belong to her alone but also to her husband. In the same way, the husband's body does not belong to him alone but also to his wife. Do not deprive each other except by mutual consent and for a time, so that you may devote yourselves to prayer. Then come together again so that Satan will not tempt you because of your lack of self-control—1 Corinthians 7:3-5, *NIV*.

The only reason a married couple should *not* have sex on a regular basis should result from an inspired burden to pray together about some specific need and for a mutually-agreed period of time. When sex is neglected in a marriage, all kinds of problems can develop. The apostle Paul names one of them—lack of self-control that can foster temptation and lust beyond the God-designed realm of marriage. If husbands and wives would take these few verses seriously and fulfill their marital responsibility with an attitude of love and submission, Satan would not be able to create sexual incompatibility in their relationship.

Because of man's depraved nature, he has taken sex and twisted, distorted, and perverted it. Some people have exploited it for money, and others have made it shameful and disgraceful because of the way they have used it. The Bible makes it clear, however, that sex is not a shameful matter. Genesis tells us, "The man and his wife were both naked, and they felt no shame" (Genesis 2:25, *NIV*). Sex in its proper place is a beautiful and wonderful experience, not something to be embarrassed about.

The Bible says in Proverbs, "Rejoice in the wife of your youth . . . may her breasts satisfy you always, may you ever be captivated by her love" (Proverbs 5:18-19, *NIV*). When the beauty and purity of sex are experienced as God intended—within the confines of the marital relationship—it produces the most profound satisfaction and the most meaningful human relationship known to man. God created this one-flesh relationship to be the height of ecstasy and physical intimacy, as well as the deepest expression of spiritual oneness between husband and wife.

A Different Approach

A man's sex drive, his potency, is essential to the perpetuation of the human race. Without it mankind would cease to exist, and the earth would be depopulated in one generation. But the ability to enjoy sexual pleasure is absolutely unnecessary to a woman for the perpetuation of the human species. Dr. Marie Robinson, a medical doctor and psychoanalyst has made in-depth studies in this area of sexual frigidity. A woman may be, as Dr. Robinson says, as frigid as a polar icecap, give birth to twenty-five children, hate every minute of it, and make her husband, herself, and her children miserable in the process.

Because her sexual pleasure is not essential to the continuance of the species, the sexuality of a woman is very delicate. Like a small tree planted with fragile roots, the winds of error and heresy can destroy that tree. This has happened to millions of women, leaving them deprived of their birthright, miserable in their marriages, and unfulfilled as women. The bitter harvest of this distortion in the

American female is ghastly to behold. It has produced frustration, bitterness, dissatisfaction, discontent in the home, and, in many cases, divorce.

Satan works in devious ways and attacks women where they are weakest. He likes to take advantage of this vulnerable area by psychological blockage of one sort or another to rob women of their sexuality. His evil purpose is not simply to make women miserable but to destroy their relationship with their husbands—especially in marriages where the husband is not a Christian. Satan likes to produce a situation where a spiritless man and sexless woman live together in hell on earth. The result creates further rebellion in the husband against God and hypocrisy in the wife against the clear teaching of Scripture.

After years of trying to help women with this problem of frigidity, a Christian psychologist on the west coast has been using a different approach. When he counsels women who say they are unable to enjoy sexual relations, his advice goes something like this:

"You are refusing to accept God's statement that your femaleness is good and that your husband's sex drive is there for a purpose. What I want you to do is go home and *repent*. That's right! Repent of the heretical attitudes that you have had toward the Word of God. Repent of the distortions and denials of your sexuality. Stop striving to compete with your husband, and repent of the animosity that exists between you and the hostility that keeps you from yielding to him. Ask God to forgive you so you can experience the deepest and most profound oneness that God meant for your marriage."

This psychologist said he was amazed at the number of women who came back to report that their lives and marriages had been transformed after their hearts and minds were made right with God.

Ladies, if you want to be liberated, let me introduce to you the greatest Liberator of all times—Jesus Christ. He can set you free to be a woman in the highest sense of the word—to know why you were created, who you are, and how to experience the fullness of your birthright. He can forgive you of your sins and take away your feelings of inferiority and hostility. If you ask for His help, Jesus can enable you to experience the satisfaction, pleasure, and fulfillment that God intended for marriage partners to enjoy. Don't let Satan deceive you in this area.

What about you husbands? If I were to ask your wife, "How is your sex life?" what would she say? Are you approaching her with gentleness and an honest concern for her needs? Do you see sex as a holy, pure, and glorious expression of your love before God? Do you pray about this most important area of your marital responsibilities? Have you experienced the intimacy of soul and of body that God wants you to have—one flesh, one spirit, one mind?

Husbands need to realize that sex is a high and holy privilege that must be approached in a tender and compassionate way in order to experience the full rewards of the marriage relationship. Wives need to see clearly that they have been deceived by the devil and robbed of what was inherently meant to be theirs by their Creator.

God's physical and spiritual ideal is for husband and wife to be one in a love relationship that leaves no room for competition, animosity, fear, guilt, or envy. If your marriage needs help, then seek it and you will find it. Almost every case of sexual incompatibility can be cured. Often simply a helpful book or a skillful counselor can unlock doors that have long separated husbands and wives from the rich fulfillment that is their birthright.

Father, help us to experience the full extent of our birthright. May we come to know the blessings You have poured out upon us in Christ and all You have created for us to enjoy. We ask this in the name of Jesus Christ, our Lord. Amen.

8

TURNING THE TIDE

Town and Country magazine once made a study of the presidents of one hundred top corporations in America. What did they find? A picture of swinging executives shuffling from one wife to another, always looking for a new model? No! They found that these successful, corporate presidents had a divorce rate of only 5 percent. The study concluded that, perhaps, marriage might not be that bad after all. In fact, it may even contribute to one's success.

Few people would argue against the benefits of marriage. Even those who get divorced have a tendency to marry again. What we have in America today differs little from the pagan polygamy that exists in some uncivilized parts of the world. In our modern society, however, *serial polygamy* is practiced—a man may have many wives, or a woman may have many husbands—they just have them one at a time.

The Futurist magazine said if the present trend continues, divorce will soon be the manner in which most marriages end. The final result of getting married will be getting divorced. What a tragic prediction! Should we as Christian husbands and wives be concerned about this current trend?

Edward Gibbon, in his monumental work, *The Decline and Fall of the Roman Empire,* said that one of the principal reasons for the dissolution of Rome was the prior dissolution of the families within it. From the time Romulus and Remus established that city on the seven hills, there was only one divorce in its five hundred year history.

Then the law was changed, and divorce became more accessible and more acceptable in the eyes of Roman society. As families began to crumble, the foundation of the Roman Empire gave way. Before long, hordes of barbarians swept down from the north; and Rome, weakened and corrupt from within, fell to her enemies.

After the Pilgrim population reached 70,000 in this country, there were six divorces over the next seventeen years—one-third of one divorce per year. During the colonial period, the divorce rate worsened, with one divorce out of every five hundred marriages. By 1812 one out of every 110 marriages ended in divorce.

One author, writing during World War II, said the alarming increase in the number of divorces in America brought on by the war would have serious effects on our society in the future. When he made that statement, there were relatively few divorces by today's standards. During the forties the total number of divorces was in the tens of thousands. By 1959, the author's worst fears had come to pass with 395,000 divorces that year. In 1961, there was one divorce for every 3.7 marriages, and by 1979, the number had climbed to 1.8 million divorces a year. Today, in California, there is one divorce for every marriage.

If Rome fell when the family was dissolved, what do we in America have to look forward to?

Whose Business Is It Anyway?

A young couple came to Dr. Louis Evans some years ago and said, "Well, Dr. Evans, we think our marriage might go on the rocks, but after all, that is definitely *our* business." Millions of people today would echo that same sentiment— that divorce is a private matter and not the business of the church, the society, or the nation. But is it? Is divorce merely a personal matter? Dr. Evans' reply to that couple was, "Your marriage is everybody's business!"

In his book, *Your Marriage: Duel or Duet?,* Dr. Evans says, "Marriage is a *nation's* business." A great pier that juts out into the midst of the ocean is pounded relentlessly by huge waves. If one piling of that pier gives way, one after another will soon crumble until the entire pier finally collapses into the angry waters. According to Dr. Evans, the same principle holds true for marriage and society. A nation is only as strong as the individual marriages and families on which it is built.

Three hundred years ago Jonathan Edwards, a dynamic Calvinistic preacher, was largely responsible for the Great Awakening in this country. His famous sermon, "Sinners in the Hands of an Angry God," brought thousands of people to Christ. Edwards was also the most original and outstanding philosopher America ever produced. His father was one of the founders of Yale University.

Jonathan Edwards married a godly woman, and over the past three hundred years his descendants have included: 265 college graduates, twelve college presidents, sixty-five university professors, sixty physicians, one hundred clergymen, seventy-five army officers, eighty prominent authors, one hundred lawyers, thirty judges, eighty public officials, three Congressmen, two United States Senators, and one Vice President of the United States.

Sociologists have compared the effects of Jonathan Edwards' life and marriage to another man living at the same time: Max Juke—a derelict and ungodly vagabond who married a woman of similar character. Over the generations, their union produced: three hundred children who died in infancy, 310 professional paupers, 440 crippled by disease, fifty prostitutes, sixty thieves, seven murderers, and fifty-three assorted criminals of other varieties.

How can anyone conclude that the quality of a marriage is a personal matter? Every marriage and every family, in one way or another, affects the strength of our nation.

At least 50 percent of all children born this year will see their parents divorced, adding a significant number to the millions of children who already come from broken homes. Psychologists tell us that the disintegration of a child's personality can almost always be traced back to the breakup of the home. Personality disintegration in a child can later lead to alcoholism, delinquency, and crime. In our nation an overwhelming number of violent crimes are committed by young people. Whose business is that?

Divorce affects not only society but the church as well. When one couple in a church gets divorced, others are immediately infected, and they begin to think, "If the problems in our marriage get too tough, we can always get a divorce like Mr. and Mrs. So-and-so."

Every divorce within the church family weakens the entire church as a moral force in the nation. Its example is sullied; the power of its influence is reduced; and its opportunities to reconcile men to Christ is diminished. Divorce then moves far beyond the personal to affect the nation, the church, and the eternal destiny of thousands of people.

Just A Piece Of Paper?

Someone said to me recently, "Marriage is nothing but a piece of paper." This kind of attitude lowers marriage to the level of a business agreement that can be cancelled any time the two partners change their minds. No wonder the divorce rate is so high in our country. "I take thee to be my lawfully wedded wife, as long as it feels good." Many people repeat the marriage vows, but 50 percent of them really mean " 'til divorce us do part."

Our society has been called the "me" generation, seeking mainly the gratification of one's own desires and pleasures. This kind of thinking is the ultimate expression of humanism and the total denial of the teachings of Christ.

Marriage, however, cannot withstand the "me" philosophy. *Current Trends* magazine said, "The search for self-gratification is inconsistent with the commitment and discipline involved in building a permanent marriage."

Dr. Kinsey, after talking to thousands of people, said that the number one element necessary for a successful marriage was *a determination and commitment to make the relationship succeed.*

Marriage, as an institution, was ordained by God and created before the church was established or before governments were formed. Because God ordained marriage, it cannot be dissolved by man. Jesus said, "What therefore God hath joined together, let not man put asunder" (Matthew 19:6). The Bible makes it clear that there are only two grounds for divorce: One is *adultery,* and the other is the irremediable *desertion* of a believer by an unsaved partner.

A judge in New York City once gave these instructions to jurors who were deciding a divorce case: "Ladies and gentlemen of the jury, you should clearly understand that we have nothing to do with the religious or sacramental aspects of this marriage. We are only dealing with the laws of the State of New York. These people are bound together by God, and that bond is not to be touched by what we do here today. They will be as married in the sight of God when we finish our work as they were before we began. And many people fail to understand that fact."

In Malachi 2:16, we read God's opinion on the matter: " 'I hate divorce,' says the Lord God of Israel." Every time a couple decides to get a divorce, they should receive a letter saying, "I hate divorce," signed: *Jehovah, God and Judge of the universe, before whom every man and woman will one day stand.*

Innumerable books have been written on the subject of divorce. Classes have discussed the problem, and counseling sessions have tried to get to the heart of the matter. But too often these futile attempts have been like the ambulance that arrives after the car has gone off the road and crashed on the rocks below. Instead of being among the ambulances and hearses at the bottom of the cliff, let's try to build a safety rail around the road at the top and help prevent the tragedy of divorce.

God's Safeguard

God created and ordained marriage, but He did not leave it without safeguards. To protect and guard the sanctity of the highest earthly relationship man can know—the one between husband and wife—God gave a specific commandment: "Thou shalt not commit adultery" (Exodus 20:14). This eighth of the ten commandments was given to purify and protect the procreation of life.

The command is simple, unqualified, irrevocable, and negative: "Thou shalt *not* commit adultery." No reason is given, as in some of the other commandments. So destructive and damning is the sin involved that no argument is necessary. Since marriage is the most basic of human relationships from which all others—the family, the church, the state—are built up, it is essential that the husband/wife relationship be jealously guarded from every form of attack.

In His teachings recorded in the gospels, Jesus hits hard at the source of the problem, taking His commands beyond law. "You have heard that it was said, 'Do not commit adultery.' But I tell you that anyone who looks at a woman lustfully has already committed adultery with her in his heart" (Matthew 5:27-28, *NIV*). The lustful look—the sin of the heart—is condemned because "out of the heart come evil thoughts . . . adultery, sexual immorality . . . " (Matthew 15:19, *NIV*). No wonder the Bible tells us to guard our hearts and our minds.

I am amazed at the attitude of professing Christians and how lightly they regard this extremely dangerous sin of *lust*. In this land, overrun with pornographic magazines, books, and motion pictures, it is vital for everyone, especially young people, to avoid the snare of lust and to flee, as the Scripture says. (See 2 Timothy 2:22.) Most women see this as a male problem, but immodest women contribute to the lust of men by the clothes they wear.

Sexual immorality is a particularly serious sin. All other sins are outside of ourselves, but the Scripture says, "He who sins sexually sins against his own body" (1 Corinthians 6:18, *NIV*). For this reason, immorality damages the human spirit and produces traumatic consequences for the individuals involved.

The tragedy of adultery is that it also affects others. It is a sin against the other spouse and breaks the conjugal vows made before God and men: "Forsaking all others, I choose thee." It is also a sin against the children, creating half-orphans who are denied the security of growing up in a home with both a father and a mother.

Not only is adultery a sin against the individual, the other spouse, and the children, it is primarily a sin against God. When a Christian commits adultery, he joins Christ—who lives within—to a harlot. (See 1 Corinthians 6:15.) God will not tolerate immorality, and the consequences of His anger are eternal. "The works of the flesh are manifest which are these; adultery, fornication, uncleanness, lasciviousness . . . they which do such things shall not inherit the kingdom of God" (Galatians 5:19,21).

In the Old Testament, when a person transgressed a law of God, they were instructed to bring certain sacrifices to obtain God's forgiveness. There were two sins, however, for which no sacrifice—and no forgiveness—was stipulated: murder and adultery. The penalty was death. In the New Testament, through Jesus Christ, we can find forgiveness of sins for which, under the Mosaic law, there was no forgiveness.

Identifying The Problem

What actually causes divorce? Psychological problems? Incompatibility? The wrong genes? What is the real problem? Most people don't like to talk about it, but the Bible makes it very clear. The reason for divorce is *sin*.

Jesus said that the law allowed the Israelites to put away their wives because of the hardness of their hearts. (See Matthew 19:8.) Hardness of heart is a direct result of sin.

79

Some of you, having heard the Word of God, know that you are guilty of adultery, immorality, lust, and uncleanness. You know you are living in sin.

Most of you, however, have been faithful to your spouse, but other sins are destroying your marriage. The sin of selfishness is a real marriage killer. How about the sin of criticism, anger, and unresolved hostility? Being unloving, unappreciative, impatient, unkind, or the sin of seeking your own instead of your mate's well-being—all these sins drive husbands and wives apart.

Sin causes divorce, but the Good News is: *Sin can be forgiven.* God loves you, and He wants to free you from the bondage and heartache of sin. Get alone with God and His Word, and let the Holy Spirit speak to you concerning the hidden sin in your life. If you acknowledge your sin and repent of it, Jesus Christ by His shed blood will cleanse you and forgive you of your sin. (See 1 John 1:7-9.)

God wants you to live an abundant, fulfilling life. With the help of the Holy Spirit, you can live victoriously over the sins of the flesh.

Committed To Change

"Okay, I won't get a divorce," you may say. "But what about my spouse? He (or she) will never change. I guess I'll just grin and bear it."

You may be able to bear it, but one thing you won't do is *grin.* This kind of attitude denies the very reason Jesus Christ died for our sin—so God, by His Spirit can change us and make us more like His Son. Receiving forgiveness for your sin is only the beginning of healing for your marriage. Although sin is the basic cause of divorce, repentance and forgiveness must be followed by a firm commitment to improve the marriage relationship.

In order to prevent divorce, our concept of marriage needs to be revamped. We need to understand that marriage is a holy relationship, chosen by Christ to represent the relationship between Himself and His Church. Because marriage was ordained by God, His blessing on that union is absolutely essential. Without God at work in a marriage, it will not succeed.

Although one in every two married couples ends up divorced, certain categories of marriages have a much higher success rate. A national survey revealed that when two criteria are present—the couple attends church; and they pray together at home—there was only one divorce in one thousand marriages. Sounds like pretty good odds to me!

Many marriages fail because husbands and wives forget the importance of having God in the center of their relationship. The simple basics of praying together, reading and sharing God's Word, and attending church as a family are left out of their marriage. If you try to build a marriage around each other, around the children, or around some common interest, it will disintegrate. A successful marriage must be built on Jesus Christ.

Before the problems in your marriage can be solved, you need to commit yourselves to the task of improving your relationship. You need to say to one another, "Come what may, we are going to work out our problems and stay together." Unless you are determined to work *through* to a solution, change will never take place.

Every marriage needs change; there is no perfect marriage. Constant growth reflects a healthy relationship. Commit yourselves to developing oneness by sharing your lives— talk openly with one another, do things as a couple, and spend time alone together. If you make a determined effort to do these things, you will be surprised at the change that will take place in your relationship.

You and your spouse may not be able to change yourselves, but God can change you. By His grace and the power of His Spirit, God can take cold hearts and confused minds and forge them in the "one" He ordained when He created male and female.

We can turn the tide of divorce—one marriage at a time.

O God, some reading this book are ensnared by the sins of sexual immorality and are helpless in their bondage. Lord, set them free. May shackles be broken as they come to the cross to be cleansed by the blood of the Lamb and to be made new by the power of Your Spirit. Help them to walk in freedom through Jesus Christ. Father, by the power of Your Spirit, change us and make us more like Jesus. Even as Christ is one with the Church in that mystical union, may we be committed to being one with our wives and husbands in that sacred institution of marriage. We invite You, O Lord, into our relationship to make it all You intended it to be. In Jesus' name. Amen.

9

PRINCIPLES FOR A SUCCESSFUL MARRIAGE

"Love is friendship set to music." I like that, don't you? In a marriage, however, the orchestration sometimes turns sour making the melody thin and strained. The harmony disappears and is replaced by a virtual cacophony of discord.

This was true of the angry wife who said to her hen-pecked husband, "Harry, are all men fools?" Meekly, he replied, "No my dear, some are still bachelors." Not much music in that marriage! In fact, I would say that very little friendship exists between them. Like musicians who must spend years studying and practicing, marriage partners must exert a great deal of effort to make their relationship a symphony of love.

Many marriages need a tune-up. If we neglect our cars, they begin to chug and jerk until we finally realize that a tune-up is needed. Sometimes, however, more serious repairs are required.

Several years ago, I purchased a shiny new Pontiac. Shortly thereafter, I parked it at Howard Johnson's where I had gone for lunch. As I was leaving the restaurant, a policeman came up to me and said, "Is that your car over there?" He was pointing to a car about thirty feet from where I had parked. The car was facing in the opposite direction, and it was a wreck.

I replied, "No, sir, my car is new. It's over. . . . It's. . . . Well, I guess that *is* my car!" It seems a lady looking for her car's brake had found the accelerator instead, leaped the curb, and done terminal damage to my new automobile. When I looked in the backseat and saw the hump that covers the drive shaft turned at a 45° angle to one of the back wheels, I knew my car had had it!

Perhaps you feel your marriage is like that car. Before you can work on tuning up the engine, you need to straighten out the framework. The rusted-out wrecks of many marriages litter the landscape, and those that still function often rattle and scrape along.

Suppose the government decided to put restrictions on owning a vehicle, and each family was allowed to purchase only one. You couldn't replace it or sell yours and buy another—that was the only car you would ever own. Do you think you would maintain that car any differently than you care for the one you presently own?

If you realize that your marriage is a permanent, once-and-for-all, indissoluble relationship that cannot be broken or replaced, would that make any difference to you? When we become convinced that marriage is a lifetime arrangement, we will cherish that relationship like a precious and prized possession, making sure it is constantly in tune and that every part is in good working order.

Raising Your Standards

We are deluged on every side with an avalanche of concepts and examples completely contrary to God's ideal for marriage. Television constantly beams them into our homes. From the Flintstones to the Honeymooners, we are given one example after another of how a marriage ought *not* to be. Stop and think about it. Almost every sitcom dealing with the family is a lesson in how to have an ungodly, unchristian marriage. If you look to the media— magazines, newspapers, radio, and TV—plus the examples of friends, family, and neighbors—your view of marriage will be warped and far removed from the standard that God expects.

84

A young man named Philip Henry fell in love and sought the hand of the daughter and heiress of Mr. Matthews of Broad Oak, England. The father, however, was sceptical, saying that although Philip was an excellent preacher and a fine gentleman, his ancestry was unknown. He told his daughter, "We do not know whence he came."

"True," his daughter replied, "but I know where he is going, and I would like to go with him." So they prevailed upon the father, and the marriage was consummated.

Twenty years later Philip Henry wrote these words in his diary: "This day we have been married twenty years, in which time we have received of the Lord twenty thousand mercies—yet though we have been married so long, we have never been reconciled for there was never any occasion for it."

Can you say that about your marriage? To the extent that you *cannot* say those words—to that extent your marriage has fallen short of what God meant it to be.

Incidentally, the great Bible scholar, Matthew Henry, was an offspring of that loving relationship. It has been said that you cannot read Matthew Henry's works without getting on your knees, so close will he bring you to the throne of God.

I read about a couple celebrating their fiftieth wedding anniversary. When the husband was asked to say a few words, he made this comment, "Fifty years ago we came to the altar of God and were joined together in holy matrimony as one. We determined right then that every morning and night we would kneel beside our bed and pray together. We would pray *with* each other and *for* each other. In fifty years, not one harsh word or even one harsh look has passed between us." How many husbands and wives can say that about their marriage?

I believe God intended marriage to be a depth of communion, a height of fellowship, and a breadth of love beyond anything we have ever known in this world. We have cheated ourselves by accepting a third rate concept of the marital relationship. It's time to expose the phony image the devil has set before us—one that has produced untold misery in countless homes—and lift our eyes to God's elevated standard of marriage. You and your mate *can* become one in Christ.

Ultimate Oneness

Most of us have never even dimly seen or conceived what God meant a Christian marriage to be. Unless you have the power of Jesus Christ in your lives, I am convinced that your relationship can never be what God intended. Spiritual oneness of heart is absolutely necessary to a successful marriage. Without it, the true meaning of marriage will elude you.

God has designed marriage to be a oneness of *mind,* a oneness of *emotions,* a oneness of *body,* and a oneness of *spirit.* Unless these exist in your marriage, your relationship is out of tune and you are not "one flesh" as God purposed. Couples who consider sex the ultimate expression of oneness often feel dissatisfied because they try to have physical unity when no spiritual, emotional, or mental oneness has preceded it. The special unity between a husband and wife is more than a conjunction of bodies.

As long as a couple is divided at the very core of their being—if the most important aspect of life is not shared as husband and wife—how can there ever be that deep communion of spirit and mind that makes two people truly one? Although they are living together as man and wife, they will invariably be going in two different directions and will never know marriage as God designed it.

People are like millstones. When a man and a woman get married, they bring a lot of rough edges to their wedding day. Before marriage, they had never been close enough to another millstone to rub off the coarse areas of their lives. But soon they begin to grind on each other—and it hurts. They squeal and yell, not realizing that God is working to perfect them. Many husbands and wives are quick to give up, take their rough edges, and run. But couples who allow the coarseness to be worn down and smoothed out are more likely to stick together and have a successful marriage.

Dr. Joseph Henry gives an excellent illustration of this in his book, *Fulfillment in Marriage*. He said that during the second world war, two physics graduate students heard their professor say that someday a method would be devised for polishing glass that would replace steel as the flattest surface known to man. When this was done, he said, a revolution in technology would take place.

After graduation, these two young physicists formed a partnership and set out to prove their professor's theory. They established a laboratory and went to work. Several years later, after a very complicated process, they had a great breakthrough. They produced such a flat surface that it could be used to measure objects within two-millionth of an inch—a great improvement over anything previously developed.

When Dr. Henry visited their plant, one of the owners said to him, "See these two squares of glass? They have been put through this new process, and I want to show you something." Then he simply placed the two pieces together, handed them to Dr. Henry, and said, "Now take them apart." After he pulled, pushed, twisted, turned and exerted all of his strength, Dr. Henry still couldn't budge them.

The young physicist explained, "Two surfaces are held together by a certain number of points of contact, but ordinarily there are so few that they easily come apart. The points on these two pieces of glass, however, have been ground down until they are almost completely flat surfaces. They are held together by so many points of contact that it is almost impossible to get them apart."

If you let God rub down the rough edges in you and your spouse, nothing will be able to tear you apart. The grinding may hurt for a while, but I urge you to surrender to God's purpose in your life. The problem in marriage is always the same: *sin*. Like the points of a porcupine, sin keeps people apart. Sin always divides, and love always draws together. Only the love of Christ can rub away these pointed edges and smooth them down so you can live in harmony with one another.

How To Increase Your Lifespan

Did you know that married people live longer than single people? This fact was discovered in an analysis of insurance company mortality tables. A person who has never married or is divorced or widowed—regardless of age grouping, race, or sex—will have a shorter lifespan than a married person. Single people will also succumb more easily to a number of the most prevalent fatal diseases.

Maybe that's why God says, "It is not good that the man should be alone" (Genesis 2:18). Loneliness causes stress and predisposes people to disease and death. One of the most essential elements missing from the life of a single person is the touch of a loved one. In touching, we express our care and concern for others, letting them know they are loved. Warmth is communicated through a touch, and comfort is brought.

Jesus often touched people as He ministered to them. Today, psychologists and physicians are aware of the miraculous results that sensitive, affectionate touching can bring. Physicians say it removes distress and eases anxiety in a patient. The power of the touch heals not only the body but also the soul. Touching a person calms their fears, lessens pain, and alleviates discouragement.

If touching is vital to our health and lifespan, no wonder God said a man should "cleave unto his wife: and they shall be one flesh" (Genesis 2:24). Cleaving implies the intimate, continuous kind of touching that creates oneness in the marriage relationship.

When I first began in the ministry, I decided to preach on verse twenty-four of Genesis chapter two. As a new preacher, I wanted to be very spiritual about this matter, and it bothered me that the Bible expressed cleaving in terms of the *flesh*. I thought, Wouldn't it have been more spiritual if God had said "and they shall be one spirit"? Now that sounds better—one mind, one heart, one spirit.

But God said "one flesh," and, as usual, God is right. Unless a husband and wife experience intimate contact that involves touching, caressing, and caring, they will not be one spirit or one mind or one heart. *Oneness begins with a touch.*

Coming Unglued

Dr. Ed Wheat, a physician and marriage counselor who has authored several books, conducted a marriage seminar at our church. He made an interesting observation about teenagers involved in their first infatuation. When a young man and woman fall in love, they act like they are stuck together with super-glue. You cannot keep them apart. When you see them driving down the street, it looks like only one person is in the car. No matter where they go, they are constantly holding hands. If their hands unclasp, their arms go around the shoulders.

Dating or engaged couples are always touching one another, and this creates that ecstatic feeling of romantic love. Then these love birds get married, and two years later you see them driving down the street with enough room between them to fit an elephant! Next thing you know they are visiting a marriage counselor. "Pastor, it's just not there anymore. I don't feel the flutter; the romance is gone."

What happened? *They came unglued.* Now they practically never hold hands, and it's been a year since he put his arm around her. About the only time they touch is when they have sex, and even that seems to have lost its glow.

Oneness without touching is impossible. The word "cleave" refers to a concept of gluing two pieces of wood together. You can put glue on both pieces, let it dry for the proper amount of time, but they won't stick together if they do not touch one another. Many marriages are being precariously held together by glue that has dried up and lost its adhesiveness. Couples must *cleave* if they are to be one.

Cleaving is different from the mechanical motion of petting Fido on the head and saying, "Nice dog, go away." That kind of touching should be reserved for those with fur and tails—not for a husband and wife who love one another.

I often hear wives say, "The only time he ever shows me any affection is when he wants sex." Mutually initiated non-sexual touching—caressing, hugging, sharing of life one with another—is essential to a healthy marriage relationship. Some married people become preoccupied with sex because they are really seeking the warmth, reassurance, and affection that comes from intimate touching. Husbands and wives need sensitive caressing not necessarily related to sex but involving the kind of affection that says to your spouse, "God has made you mine, and I will love you all my days."

A line from an old familiar song contains some good advice: "Hug him every morning and kiss him every night, for a good man, nowadays, is hard to find." That's even more true today. But a good woman is equally hard to find, and she needs that special touch of affection from her husband. A married person who fails to receive affectionate touching from their mate can be just as lonely as someone who is single.

Rekindling The Romance

How about your marriage? Do you and your spouse have the same intimate oneness that existed when you were dating? Compare the amount of touching you did then to the amount that you now experience. Are you cleaving the way God says you should? Or are you and your mate like two plastic bubbles rolling around the house, occasionally bumping into one another as you go your separate ways with no cleaving, no oneness, and no feeling of intimacy?

Many people have a warped idea of love and marriage. They think you fall in love, get engaged, and a wonderful feeling of romantic love fills your heart. Then you get married, and the romantic love gradually fades away over the next few years as you go about raising children, making a household, earning a living, etc. But Dr. Wheat says that is not God's plan at all. God expects the feeling of romantic love, excitement, and ecstacy to grow throughout marriage.

How can you keep that feeling of love and romance alive in your relationship with your husband or wife? Dr. Wheat says, "Nothing can build or rebuild an intense feeling of love in a marriage as responsive touching, reaching out to a responding partner."

The renewal of love begins with a decision of the will that says, "I will reach out, as Jesus did, to touch and heal and restore my marriage." The action of reaching out to your spouse expresses your love in a way nothing else can. Dr. Wheat says, "The more freely you express your affection in physical terms of touching and pleasuring the other, the more love you will 'feel' for your marriage partner."

I cannot overemphasize the importance of sensitive, affectionate touching, but I can include what Dr. Wheat tells married couples who read his book, *Love Life For Every Married Couple:* "If you practice everything else in this book, but do not touch each other frequently and lovingly, the thrill of romantic love will be absent from your marriage." Don't miss out on this God-given blessing.

Developing Spiritual Unity

Although your marriage may never be perfect, you can achieve far beyond what most people ever dream is possible. That high and lofty ideal of marriage—one man and one woman joined together for life in a holy, indissoluble, intimate relationship of oneness—should be the goal set before you and your mate.

Spiritual unity is the key to oneness in marriage. The closer you draw to Jesus—the One who breaks down the barriers of sin that separate and divide—the closer you will draw to one another. The farther you move away from Jesus, the greater the gap between you and your mate.

Maintaining that personal relationship with Jesus Christ requires spending time talking with Him in prayer—and in listening to His voice as He speaks to you from God's Word. As your faith and trust in God are developed, you will become more sensitive to your mate and better able to meet his or her needs. When both spouses know Jesus Christ as Savior, they share a spiritual unity that binds them together in love the way nothing else can.

The basic principle of a successful marriage is love. "For God so loved, He gave. . . . " Love is giving of yourself to your spouse and desiring to put his or her needs before your own. Love requires a conscious effort to please your husband or wife and make their life as happy, pleasant, and peaceful as you possibly can. Open yourself to Jesus Christ—the source of all love—and ask Him to come into your heart and fill you with His love.

God in Jesus Christ has not only given us marriage as a high and holy ideal; but, by the power of His Word and His Holy Spirit, He has given us the strength to reach for that ideal.

Acres Of Diamonds

Remember the story I told in the introduction about the acres of diamonds? If you want to discover the hidden "diamonds" in your marriage relationship, you must possess two qualities. First, you must have *perseverance*—don't give up even when it looks like you've found worms instead of jewels. Secondly, *mutual effort* must be exercised by both partners. It is unrealistic to think you will discover anything if you let your husband or wife do all the digging while you lean comfortably on your shovel. Get in there and get your hands dirty; dig down and pull out the ugliness by the roots.

Failure to live according to God's high standard for marriage is to sin against the instructions of God's Word. If you willfully refuse to make an effort to improve your marital relationship, you deprive yourself and your spouse of one of the greatest sources of joy in this world. And you deny your children the best gift you can give them—a happy father and mother.

What is your marriage like: disastrous? so-so? or terrific? May God grant you the desire and priority in your life to apply God's principles to your relationship with your husband or wife. Decide today that you are going to discover the treasure that had been hidden from you: those "acres of diamonds" right in your own backyard.

Father, may the Holy Spirit work to soften our hearts toward one another so we can realize our own sinfulness and determine to show Your love to our mate. Forgive us for the many sins, slights, and selfishness that keep us apart as husband and wife. Grant us a new view of marriage— the oneness that Christ alone can give. May His Spirit of love fill our hearts and help us to experience the depth of oneness and the height of communion that You desire for us to know. We pray that Jesus Christ may be glorified in our marriage relationship. In His name. Amen.

Let me pray for you and your marriage.

Heavenly Father, send Your Holy Spirit to move in the hearts of the husbands and wives reading this book. Cause them to be committed to the principles of marriage found in Your Word. May the communion of their lives enjoy the richness of the promises of God. In Jesus' name. Amen.

Part Two

LEARNING TO LIVE WITH YOUR CHILDREN

10

PARENTS AND CHILDREN

Whatever happened to the old maxim, "Children are to be seen and not heard"? We live in a day when children are making themselves heard and speaking their minds.

When Johnny brought home a not-too-good report card, his father admonished him with these words, "Do you realize that when George Washington was your age, he was making straight A's?" Was Johnny now properly admonished and determined to do better? Not exactly. His response was, "Yeah, Pop, and when he was your age, he was President of the United States!"

Although little four-year-old Cathy was generally a good little girl who went to Sunday School and always knew her memory verse, she had her rebellious moments. As punishment for being naughty, her parents set her dinner on a TV tray in the corner and seated her facing the wall. Having been taught to pray before her meal, Cathy folded her hands and said, "Thou preparest a table before me in the presence of mine enemies."

These stories appear humorous on the surface, but they are actually subtle indicators of the younger generation's attitude toward those in authority over them. Many children have the feeling that parents are the enemy—a foe to be opposed, intimidated, threatened, and overcome. The relationship between children and parents has degenerated over the years, creating a widening gap between the generations.

A whole generation of young people is turned off and tuned out to their parents, wanting nothing to do with them and the value system they represent. Words like alienation, animosity, frustration, anger, and rebellion describe the attitude fostered by television and movies. It's not unusual to hear a teenager tell his hardworking, responsible father, "I hate your guts."

Throughout the country there is an alarming rise in teenage alcoholism and drug abuse. Premarital sex is rampant even among early teens. Rock music promotes rebellion and anarchy. Why are we having such problems with our young people?

The Discipline Gap

For the past thirty-five to forty years we have been creating an undisciplined generation with the help of psychologists and teachers who promoted a permissive method of childrearing. We were told that spanking a child was a barbaric and uncivilized way for an intelligent modern parent to act. Dr. Spock taught a whole generation of parents to spare the rod and spoil the child, and millions leaped to follow his instruction. The permissive school of thought told us today's children have been too closely restricted and disciplined. The answer is to let them do their own thing.

We have created a whole new generation of young people who have no respect for authority. And it all began in the home with parents who were more inclined to believe ungodly teachers and psychologists than the Word of God.

By heeding the advice of these progressive educators, we have raised, to a large extent, a generation of moral misfits, juvenile delinquents, student drug pushers, and rebellious teenagers. In some cities, it has been estimated that over 90 percent of the high school students are now or have been on drugs. Many teachers fear for their lives and their safety in the classroom.

My own brother, a former high school teacher, told me that he once bought a new world map and set it up in front of his class. When my brother asked a question of a six-foot-two, two-hundred-twenty-pound student who didn't know the answer, the kid stood up, walked to the front of the class, pulled out a six-inch switchblade, and carved the map into pieces. Then he turned to my brother and said, "Any other questions, teach?" After that experience, my brother took up weight lifting to prevent further harassment. This happened in a small Florida town. Can you imagine what it must be like in the big cities?

The scenario is frightening. A college president disciplined a student for violating school policy. The next day, the young man walked into the president's office and shot him dead.

I have had parents tell me they are afraid of their children. Recently I read about a teenager who took an ax and chopped his parents into small pieces because they wouldn't let him do what he wanted. The Scripture teaches parents to chasten their children before it is too late. (See Proverbs 19:18.) In this case it was too late, not only for the child but also for the parents.

It seems that all the professional advice and instruction parents have received for the last generation and a half has only succeeded in producing young people who have learned to take matters into their own hands when they don't get their own way. Someone said, "What we have today is not a generation gap but a *discipline gap.*"

How God Sees It

Parents and children both need to hear what God has to say about disobedience and rebellion—about those who do it and those who allow it. God's Word compares rebellion to the sin of witchcraft, an abomination in His sight, that will unfailingly bring its practitioner down into the pit of hell. (See 1 Samuel 15:23.) The consequences are clear: "Woe to the rebellious childen" (Isaiah 30:1).

The main reason our young people are rebelling the way they are today is because the adults are allowing it. They are not only allowing it; they are condoning it! Some are even applauding it!

God has much to say about parents who allow this sort of thing to happen. Rebellion among our young people will continue until parents and adults in positions of authority realize it is our responsibility to stop it. The first place to stop rebellion is in the home. Then it needs to be continued in the school.

We, as parents, need to make it clear to our children at home what our responsibility before God is and what theirs is. We need to make it clear to our teachers, to our schools, and to all those in authority over our children just how we feel about this matter. As long as we remain silent, we will be like Eli, who pampered his children and brought them and himself down to destruction. (See 1 Samuel 2:12-36.)

What about the Bible—this old book that has been rejected by most modern psychologists and educators? It is interesting to note that the rise in juvenile problems corresponds to the decline in the application and belief in the Scriptures. Most commentators and analysts of the current scene seem to be totally oblivious to this obvious correlation. But many parents, after realizing they have been led astray, are rediscovering the Bible. Even secular psychologists are proposing the same principles that have been taught in the scriptures for centuries.

Let's look at what God's Word has to say about the child's duty and the parents' responsibility.

The Child's Duty

When the apostle Paul writes about the relationship and responsibilities of children and parents, he speaks first to the children: "Children, obey your parents in the Lord, for this is right. 'Honor your father and mother'—which is the

100

first commandment with a promise—'that it may go well with you and that you may enjoy long life on the earth' " (Ephesians 6:1, *NIV*).

The first duty of a child is to obey his parents. The naturally rebellious nature of children, however, struggles against being submissive and obedient to their parents. When children are left to do "what comes naturally," chaos results. Mothers and fathers have been provided by God to protect, train, and rear their children in the Lord. Parents, therefore, are to be obeyed because it is best for all concerned. It is the children's responsibility to obey their parents and the parents' responsibility to see that they do.

In addition to being obedient, children are also commanded to honor their parents. This means they should respect them and hold their parents in high esteem. Their tone of voice and attitude of heart should always be one of respect and honor. Children who are taught to behave this way will live a long, full life. But, the Bible says, "The eye that mocks a father, that scorns obedience to a mother, will be pecked out by the ravens of the valley" (Proverbs 30:17, *NIV*). That's a very serious judgment against a child. Parents who don't want their children to incur God's judgment must demand respect and honor from them. Then, instead of problems, their children will have an enjoyable, prosperous future ahead of them. Isn't that what you want for your children?

A young man once had a great desire to become a sailor and see the world. He decided to become a midshipman, despite his mother's urging him not to. When the time came for him to leave, he packed his trunk and went down to the dock. His mother followed him in tears. After he had put his trunk on the ship that would take him away from his mother for years, he turned to say goodbye to her. Seeing his mother with tears running down her face as she stood on the dock, he hesitated only for a moment before saying, "Stop! Put my trunk ashore. I will not sail away and break my mother's heart." His mother embraced him and said,

"Son, God has said He will honor the child who honors his parents." The name of that would-be sailor was George Washington, and God certainly kept His promise.

This command to honor our parents is unique from all others because there may come a time when we will no longer be able to obey it. With sadness we may recall all the opportunities to care for and honor our parents that we let slip by. One man said, "Oh, that I might appear in heaven for one hour before my parents and know that I have been forgiven for all the grief and pain and anguish that I caused them by my disobedience."

Are your parents gone, or do you still have the opportunity to obey this commandment? Maybe you are no longer a child who must obey your parents, but you can honor them until they leave this world. You will not be blessed if you forget the parents who gave you the life you now enjoy. Remember them and look for opportunities to show your gratitude for all they have done for you over the years. Care for their needs, and don't neglect them in their old age. Reverence and respect the position they hold as your parents. If you do, it will save you untold remorse in the years after they are gone. Besides, the personal rewards of a long, full life are certainly worth the small effort it takes to show mom and dad that they are special to you.

The Parents' Responsibility

All authority is given from God, and everyone comes under authority of one kind or another. That is how we learn to live under the authority of the Lordship of Christ. Children are placed under their parents' authority, and mom and dad must come under the authorities over them.

Earlier in Ephesians, we learned that the responsibility of the husband is to love the wife and the wife is to be in subjection to her husband. Dad must first come under Christ's authority, and mom must submit herself to her husband's authority over her.

How many mothers have lamented over their disobedient children, yet all the time they have been unwilling to be in subjection to their husbands? Or how many husbands wonder why their wives are not in subjection and their children are rebellious, when they themselves are not willing to submit to their head, who is Christ? *Rebellious parents produce rebellious children.* Before you can expect your children to obey and honor you, your own rebellious attitudes need to be brought into line with God's Word. Only then can you fulfill your God-given duty to your children.

I have known many people who have been quite proficient in their chosen occupation, but they could not get along in life because they couldn't get along with people. They moved from one job to another, weakening their family and destroying their marriage. The source of their problem can be traced back to the fact that they never learned how to submit to authority as a child—because their parents never required it of them. Those who have made a study of this matter declare that most people fail at their jobs *not* because of technical lack of knowledge but because of an inability to get along with their fellow workers, particularly those in authority over them.

A child must learn to submit himself to a higher authority. If he does not learn this as a child, it is unlikely he will later learn to submit himself to Jesus Christ who claims to be his Lord and Master. When a child develops habits of rebellion during the formative stages of his personality, these attitudes carry over into his relationships with his teachers, with his employers, and, most tragically, with his God.

Heavenly Father, help us as parents to know that an undisciplined child will produce an undisciplined life—a life in disarray, a life incapable of self-control. Help us to discipline our children so they will become Your disciples. In our homes cause the love of Christ to flow from parent to child and from child to parent to the praise and glory of Thy holy name. Amen.

11

TEACHING THEM GOD'S WAY

In the last chapter we learned that parents are responsible for raising their children according to God's principles of childrearing. What does God's Word have to say to parents today? We can summarize the Bible's instructions to parents with this command: Bring up your children "in the nurture and admonition of the Lord" (Ephesians 6:4). That means we are to *teach* and *discipline* our children according to God's Word. In this and the next chapter, we will look at these two aspects of parental responsibility.

The Buck Stops Here

Who is to teach your children? The Sunday school teacher? The pastor? The Christian school teacher? In Ephesians the command is directed to *fathers:* "Fathers, do not exasperate your children; instead, bring them up in the training and instruction of the Lord" (6:4, *NIV*).

Why is the father so instructed, when it is obviously the mother who spends more time with the child and has the most immediate and frequent opportunities for discipline and teaching? The father is away at work most of the day. Why, then, are these words directed to fathers?

The father is the head of the household and is responsible for the spiritual welfare of his family. God holds him accountable for the nurture and admonition of his children. One of the qualifications of a Christian leader is that he must "manage his own family well and see that his children obey him with proper respect. (If anyone does not know how to manage his own family, how can he take care of God's church?)" (1 Timothy 3:4-5, *NIV*).

When you manage something—whether it be your family or a business—you don't do everything yourself. You delegate authority and then see to it that your instructions are carried out. The final result is your responsibility. The buck stops with you. If your children are not properly trained and disciplined, it is the father who is held responsible by God. Fathers, are you the spiritual heads of your households?

Many fathers have turned their children over to the Sunday School for their spiritual training. They do not realize, however, that Sunday School was created in the nineteenth century to instruct orphans and the children of unbelieving parents. Good Christian parents taught their children so well at home that they didn't feel any need for formal instruction in a specially designed school. But times have changed, and today the Sunday School teacher must do in one hour on Sunday what the parents should be doing all week long. Mothers and dads are to teach the Word of God to their children, encouraging them to learn it and to hide it in their hearts.

One At A Time

What are you to teach your children? What does it mean to nurture your children in the Lord? It means to teach them the commands of God. After the Israelites were given the ten commandments, they were instructed: "These commandments that I give you today are to be upon your hearts. Impress them on your children" (Deuteronomy 6:6-7, *NIV*).

Are you familiar enough with the ten commandments to be able to teach them to your children? Do you know the commands of Christ given in the gospels? What about the specific instructions given to believers in the epistles?

In counseling with many young adults, I have found that they are not aware of the fact that fornication is a sin, and in many cases they do not even know what it is. They assume that if neither party is married, there is really nothing wrong with having sex. Scripture makes it very plain that premarital sex—fornication—is a *sin* from which Christians must abstain. (See 1 Thessalonians 4:3.) Have you taught that to your pre-teens and teenagers?

Ann Landers once related the story of a young girl, about fourteen, who had been having premarital sex with a boy her age. She wrote and asked what time of the month would be best to do this because her religion forbade her to use contraceptives. Ann Landers wrote back and said, "Your religion forbids you to do what you are doing at any time of the month." This teenager was totally ignorant of God's command. And we wonder why our young people go astray!

Have you taught your children the commandments of God? Have you seen to it that they know them? Have you taught your children the gospel of Christ? The eternal salvation of their souls lies primarily in your hands. The parent who is unable to share the gospel of Christ with his own child has no one to blame but himself when the child grows up to be a rebel.

Line Upon Line

How are parents to teach their children? The established method of instruction in Old Testament times was "Precept upon precept; line upon line, line upon line, here a little, and there a little" (Isaiah 28:10). Children were taught one command at a time, and practical instruction relating to that command was given whenever a situation presented itself. Parents, and especially fathers, were to impress God's commands on their children and "talk about them when you sit at home and when you walk along the road" (Deuteronomy 6:7).

107

If your child has a problem with taking things that don't belong to him, have him memorize a half dozen verses concerning stealing. If your child is having trouble telling the truth, teach him that God's Word puts liars in the same category as murderers and idolaters—none of whom will be in heaven. (See Revelation 21:8.) If your child has a problem with impure thoughts and actions, teach him what God has to say about the consequences of this kind of behavior. God's Spirit will take the Word and use it to transform your child's life.

If your child rebels against your authority over him, have him read with you what the Bible says about chastening and disciplining children. Have your child read the verse that says you are to chasten him if you love him, and if you don't chasten him, you hate him. (See Proverbs 13:24.) God's Word will have a tremendous effect upon the child's life and make a far greater impact than an angry lecture by dad.

Louder Than Words

In addition to verbal instruction and application, a parent's most effective method of teaching is *by example.* Children tend to learn more by what we *do* than by what we say—our lives speak louder than our words.

Are you faithful to the commands of Christ in your home? Do you apply His teachings in your relationship with your husband or your wife? Are you faithful to Christ and His church, or do you murmur and complain about serving Him?

Some parents have fried preacher every Sunday for dinner. What effect does that have on children who are at the table? I am reminded of a family in our church who had several young children. These youngsters would never leave the church without enthusiastically shaking my hand. Then their father became disenchanted about something in the church, and his children began to avoid me. Why? Because they had big ears and were hearing what was being said in the home. Soon these children would not even speak to me.

And parents wonder why their children stop going to church. Is it the church's fault or the child's fault? Maybe it is the bad example set by the parents.

Do you bring your children to Sunday School and go with them? Or do you just send them? Do you set an example for your children by studying the Word of God at home, attending Sunday School, and seeing that your children are there also? Your example of godly living will teach your children in ways a thousand sermons never could.

The way we live can have negative repercussions if what we are showing our children by our example is not consistent with what we are teaching them by our precept. A Sunday school teacher asked one young child, "Do you have prayers in your home?" He said, "Yes." Then the teacher asked, "When?" The little boy replied, "When company comes." The only thing that child is being taught is that the God worshiped in his home is the God of public opinion.

Andrew Murray, author and Christian leader during the nineteenth century, had a tremendous spiritual impact on his nation of South Africa. Many of his books have become Christian literary classics, read and loved by millions throughout the world for generations. Andrew grew up in a home with eleven brothers and sisters, each becoming a most outstanding individual. One day his mother was asked how she managed to raise eleven of the most marvelous children that had ever graced that state. She said the only thing she did was try to live before them the kind of life that she wanted them to live.

What kind of lives are we living before our children? Are we showing them an example of faithfulness, kindness, honesty, peace, and thoughtfulness? Or are we showing them an example of irritability, deceitfulness, and negativism? The child steals a lollipop and gets a spanking. Then he washes his hands and dries them on a Holiday Inn towel! And we wonder why they don't get the point! What kind of an example are you setting in your home?

You've heard it said, "A picture is worth a thousand words." Long after your words have faded into the air, a picture of your life will be instilled on the minds of your children. Will they remember dad with the Bible open before him, teaching them God's Word? Or will their most impressionable memory be of dad sitting every evening in front of the television, watching one degrading program after another? The lasting impression you leave on your children will affect them the rest of their lives. The *kind* of impression you leave is up to you.

Heavenly Father, help us as parents, and especially as fathers, to accept our God-given responsibility to teach our children Your Word and Your ways. May the example we set before them be one that will challenge them to live in a way that is pleasing to You. In Jesus' name. Amen.

12

TO LOVE IS TO DISCIPLINE

Discipline has been an ugly word for the past generation. "Never spank a child! You might bruise his ego permanently," we were told. Well, I have spanked my child a number of times, and whatever little bruises were there, I assure you, were not on the ego.

The Bible says, "He who spares the rod, hates his son, but he who loves him is careful to discipline him" (Proverbs 13:24, *NIV*). A parent who loves his child will spank him. And the parent who does not discipline him hates his child, knowingly or unknowingly. That is pretty strong language, but God said it.

God's Word says that if we use the rod, we will deliver our child from eternal death. (See Proverbs 23:14.) Isn't that an awesome responsibility? Many parents, because of the undisciplined way in which they have reared their children, have delivered them into hell forever. The undisciplined child grows up to be a rebel, refusing to submit to the authority of his parents, the authority of the school, the authority of the state, and the authority of God. Parents who listen to secular psychologists rather than to the Word of God don't realize that they may be condemning their child to eternal punishment.

Some parents are not willing to have their laid-back lifestyles disturbed with such burdensome tasks as administering discipline. "Why rock the boat? Besides, I can't stand to hear the child crying!" The Bible says not to withhold discipline from a child simply because the child is upset about being punished. (See Proverbs 23:13.)

Discipline is an outward expression of love that is consistent with the character of God. One of the ways God proves to us that we are loved and accepted by Him is His chastening of us: "The Lord disciplines those he loves, and he punishes everyone he accepts as a son. . . . For what son is not disciplined by his father? If you are not disciplined . . . then you are illegitimate children and not true sons. Moreover, we have all had human fathers who disciplined us and we respected them for it" (Hebrews 12:6-9, *NIV*).

If we, as parents, do not discipline our children, then we are ignoring the teaching of God's Word and acting contrary to His character. To find out how God chastens His children, study the Old Testament. You will discover that God always disciplines justly, lovingly, and firmly.

Your children will respect you for caring enough to take the time and effort to punish them for their wrong behavior. "No discipline seems pleasant at the time, but painful. Later on, however, it produces a harvest of righteousness and peace for those who have been trained by it" (Hebrews 12:11, *NIV*).

Isn't that what you want for your children—a righteous and peaceful life? Some day your grown children will come and thank you for making that possible in their lives.

Discipline With Love

Dr. Jay Adams wrote an excellent article on this subject. He talked to many children and asked whether they would prefer corporal punishment (that is, the paddle) to being forced to stay in their room or deprived of other privileges. The children almost unanimously said they would rather be spanked. Parents who don't spank their children think they are being merciful, yet the children feel otherwise.

During a drawn-out period of punishment, a cold, distant attitude of alienation grows between parent and child. On the other hand, if parents apply the board of education to the seat of learning, there may be tears and weeping afterwards; but when it is immediately followed by a time of embracing and reconciliation, the air is cleared and all is forgiven. For corporal punishment to be effective, it should be done in love and not in anger.

Dr. Adams says many parents (especially mothers) use what he calls the *decibel method* of discipline. A decibel discipliner just keeps raising the voice louder and louder, until finally it is lost altogether. The child, of course, soon gets used to the noise, and the parent has to scream at the child in order to get results: "Do you hear me, Johnny?"

A little boy whose mother used this method was overheard saying to his playmate, "You don't have to really do anything until she puts on her mad voice." Unfortunately, a child disciplined in this way learns to live in an atmosphere of tension and animosity. When he grows up, he becomes an angry parent who deals with his children the same way.

When speaking to children about any misbehavior, a normal tone of voice should be used by the parent. In addition, the child should not be permitted to assume the habit of whining or shouting. After the "facts of the case" have been presented by the child or children involved, the parent should calmly and reasonably explain the degree of punishment that will be meted out. If spanking is the punishment, then do it in love and with understanding. A controlled but firm manner of correction will show your children that discipline is a matter of love and not a matter of temper.

The Bible says that the fathers are not to provoke their children to wrath. (See Ephesians 6:4.) That means not only the father but anyone else who is allowed to discipline your child. The father is responsible for seeing that the mother or grandmother or babysitter does not use any method of discipline that is physically, psychologically, or emotionally harmful to the child.

The misuse of discipline occurs when a parent allows a child's misbehavior to continue until the parent loses his temper and strikes the child on the face or head. God created the human body with a proper place for the administration of discipline—the well-padded backside. To hit a child anywhere else can result in physical harm and permanent emotional scars.

In talking to children, I have discovered that many have no idea why their parents correct and punish them. They think it is because their parents are mean and don't want them to have a good time or because their parents get angry and lose their temper. We should never punish our children in anger, but we should chasten them in love.

Think back in your own childhood. Remember the spankings? Do you remember your parents telling you why they were doing it? Perhaps they were doing it for wrong reasons—impatience, anger, loss of temper. Or perhaps they were punishing you for the right reasons, but they never really told you.

As parents, we need to emphasize over and over again to our children that we are disciplining them because we love them. There is no more important time when your child needs to know you love him than when you discipline him. Instead of driving him away from you, let the child know you love him, before and after the discipline takes place.

Mistakes Parents Often Make

The Living Bible paraphrases the instruction to parents this way: "And now a word to you parents. Don't keep on scolding and nagging your children, making them angry and resentful. Rather, bring them up with the loving discipline the Lord himself approves, with suggestions and godly advice" (Ephesians 6:4, *TLB*).

Many children hear nothing from their parents but "No! No! Don't! Stop!" Everything they say and do is criticized. Children have said, "I have never done one thing in my life

114

that my parents wholeheartedly approved of. Sometimes it was better, or it was pretty good, but it was never just right." Children need our praise, our encouragement, our comfort, and our consolation.

How many parents have suffered the heartbreak of seeing their children grow up, thumb their noses at them, and walk off, never to see them again? The parents cry out in despair, "Where did I go wrong? What did I do? We gave them the best of everything." Yes, you gave them the finest clothes and the best education, but over and over you constantly found fault. All your child ever heard was, "Can't you do anything right? What's the matter with you? Do you have to drop everything you get your hands on?" Every mistake is followed by a three-part speech: What they've done before; what they are now; and what their prospects are in the future.

Children often complain that their parents won't listen to them. I must confess that I sometimes disciplined my child before I heard all of the facts about the situation. When our daughter was three years old, an incident happened that taught me to get all the facts before carrying out the punishment.

One evening I had just come home from work when my wife told me our little girl had been impossible all day long. Since I needed evidence, I waited until dinnertime to see how she would act. As soon as we sat down, she announced that she had no intention of eating her meal. Her bold defiance was too much, and I had to let her know who was in charge. I got up from the table, picked up a wide ruler, and began to ceremoniously slap it on the palm of my hand for effect. Immediately, she picked up her fork and started eating. Not a whine or a word of complaint was heard as I stood there hovering over her saying she would eat every bite. And she did.

I said to myself, "Jim, old boy, you've just got to let them know who is boss." As I turned to go back to my chair, she upchucked all over the kitchen floor! We then discovered that she hadn't wanted to eat because she wasn't feeling well. As I stood there feeling her forehead and noting the fever, I kept getting a flash of this six-foot ogre, slapping a ruler and terrorizing this ill, little girl.

Do you know what the Bible calls a person who answers a matter before he has heard it fully? The Bible calls him a *fool*. (See Proverbs 18:13.) More than once I have had to go and tell my child I was wrong and the discipline was unjust. Do you ever apologize to your child and admit that you are wrong? If you do, it will have a great effect upon your child, who will find out that you are human, too, and not above asking for forgiveness.

Keeping It Consistent

One of the greatest causes of frustration and anger among children is inconsistent discipline. One day you get murdered for nothing, and the next day you get nothing for murder. The child doesn't know what to do. Children need boundaries. Without them, children feel their parents do not love them or care for them. A home where there are no defined boundaries for expected behavior makes a child psychologically insecure.

Our heavenly Father knows how important boundaries are. God's Word makes it clear what we are to do and the result if we don't do it. Parents need to do the same thing by spelling out the family rules and the consequences for not obeying them. But that takes work. Parents must search the scriptures, pray together, and agree on the kind of behavior they feel is acceptable and unacceptable. They must then determine the kind of punishment that will be given in certain situations. The degree of punishment should always fit the "crime."

Children are very clever and will go from mom to dad, trying to play them off against each other. That's why parents must present a unified front. One rule we had in our home was if one parent made a decision, the child did not go to the other parent and try to get them to override or veto it.

Suppose the husband and wife do not agree on the kind of rules they should have. You may have talked it over and prayed about it, yet you still do not agree. Then the husband has the final say because he is the one God holds responsible. The wife, of course, must support her husband's decision.

It is the wife's responsibility to be the example of submission in the home. When the children see that their mother respects and submits to their father, they will submit to him also. At the same time, the husband must see that the children respect and obey their mother.

The Positive Side Of Discipline

In the Bible, we read that God offers a reward to children who are obedient. "Children, obey your parents in the Lord, for this is right. 'Honor your father and mother'—which is the first commandment with a promise—'that it may go well with you and that you may enjoy long life on the earth' " (Ephesians 6:1-3, *NIV*).

Christian parents should realize that rewards are a part of discipline. When children know that obedience will result in blessing, they will think twice before they disobey. Parents should offer rewards as an incentive. As children take on greater responsibilities, they should get extended privileges and higher rewards. Do you give your children rewards? Do you encourage them to achieve by rewarding them for their efforts? This is one of the most effective teaching methods.

I remember hearing Charlie Jones, a fantastic Christian man, tell how he dealt with his son when he came and asked for money. Charlie told his son that in order to get his allowance he would have to read certain books. For each book that his son read and wrote a report on, Charlie paid him a set amount. Charlie selected books that he knew would help develop his son's mind and personality. In addition, he chose books that would increase his spiritual growth and his son's commitment to Christ. Charlie had him read biographies of great missionaries and mighty men and women of God.

When Charlie's son went off to college, his father said, "I received a post card from him every day while he was in college for four years. One of the most frequently repeated statements was how much he appreciated the number of friends he had gotten to know in these books he had read over the years. He said he was far ahead of his classmates who knew nothing about this great treasure of wisdom and inspiration that he had received."

Bring up your children in the nurture and the admonition of the Lord. Share the gospel and the love of Jesus Christ with them. The most important gift you can give your children is to bring them to a genuine spiritual, saving knowledge of Christ. Unless the Spirit of God melts their hearts and takes away their rebellion, there is little hope for them once they are beyond the influence of your home and discipline. But if you have raised them with love and taught them the commands and ways of God, then you can claim this promise: "Train up a child in the way he should go: and when he is old, he will not depart from it" (Proverbs 22:6).

Heavenly Father, give us the grace we need to be better parents. Help us to accept our God-given responsibility to teach and discipline our children so that they will come to a saving knowledge of Jesus Christ. May our lives be living examples of Your love and forgiveness. We ask these things in the name of Jesus Christ. Amen.

13

AS THE TWIG IS BENT

"As the twig is bent, so grows the tree." That familiar aphorism embodies very basic scriptural and spiritual principles, teaching us that the way a life is directed and influenced in the early years is the bent it will take later. "Train up a child in the way he should go: and when he is old, he will not depart from it" (Proverbs 22:6). The responsibility for bending the twig or training the child is placed squarely upon the shoulders—not of the school or the church—but upon you, the parents.

It is the parents' responsibility to train up their children in the way they should go. But who really has the greatest influence on your children? How do they learn their values? Where do they spend most of their time during the day? If your children are over the age of five, their lives are being molded day in and day out, hour after hour at *school*.

Instead of using the Bible as the guidebook for training children, many parents rely on custom or tradition. In America that means the tradition of public education. Because of the tremendous influence the public school system has on children, I want to make parents aware of the dangers lurking behind the closed doors of their child's classroom.

Many people suppose that public schools go back to the beginning of our nation. Actually, public education is a rather novel idea in America. From the time the Pilgrims landed here in the early 1600s until the middle of the nineteenth century, most of the education in this country was provided by religious organizations. It was only in the middle of the last century that public education came into being.

The first organized protest against private and religious schools was begun in 1818 by Robert Owen, a self-proclaimed socialist. He promoted the ideal of secular, public education where socialist values could be inculcated.

For more than one hundred years, however, the public educational system in this land had a very strong Christian influence. The Bible was read freely, prayers were often heard, and teachers had a strong moral influence on the children. But all that changed when a few militant atheists realized they could use the constitution to rid our schools of God. They argued that our nation is built upon the principle of separation of church and state and, because public education is funded by the state, all religious teaching should be removed from the school.

The respected columnist, Milton Friedman, calls education "the only bastion of socialism in a sea of free enterprise in America." Where is the only bastion of socialism in America? In our public schools.

Today the Bible can no longer be read or prayers be heard in our public schools. Teachers are fearful of saying anything that may result in their dismissal. Principals are afraid of parents and liberal organizations who might file a civil suit against them and their schools. What effect has this had on our educational system? In the past twenty-five years, it has deteriorated tremendously—both morally and academically.

When God Is Ignored

With no moral or spiritual foundation, the philosophical basis of our public educational system has developed these three underpinnings: First, it is basically *materialistic* in its emphasis; the spiritual realm has been ruled, by court decree, out of academia. Secondly, it is *relativistic* as far as its view of truth is concerned; there is no absolute truth—all things are relative. Since they have no revelation from God of absolutes, truth becomes a relative matter. Thirdly, it is purely *secularistic.* All Christian teaching has been banned, and secular humanism has become the religion of public education.

Now think for a moment. What is the philosophical basis of education in Soviet Russia or Communist China? Is it not strictly materialistic? Certainly and completely relativistic? And thoroughly secularistic? The students in America's schools today are being educated, for the most part, on the same philosophical foundation as students in Russia. And we wonder why we so often have a similar product.

In our secularistic schools in America, a new mindset exists that was not prevalent in this country fifty or one hundred years ago. Life and the world are viewed without God. Students imbibe, almost as if by osmosis, a godless philosophy that views life solely on human terms and sees a world from which God has been silently, quietly, and effectively banished. When God is removed, He does not have to be denied. He simply has to be ignored.

Students study the starry heavens, not to marvel at the wonders of God's creation but to praise the magnificent mind of man who developed the high-powered telescopes and observation satellites used by scientists. Science becomes their god, and man's theories of life and creation are expounded as truth. Historical events are presented as man's stepping stones to greatness, while man's obvious failure to live at peace with his neighbor is overlooked.

Philosophers have tried for twenty-five hundred years to find a unified whole without the divine revelation of Scripture. Finally, they came to realize that it is impossible in a godless world to find any unifying meaning-giving system for thought. So, every philosopher just made up his own theory about the meaning and purpose of life.

This is the reason chaos reigns in the hearts and minds of so many young college students today. They adopt the philosophy of existentialism and conclude that life is absurd.

To them, life has no meaning. The past is irrelevant, and the future has no significance. Living for the moment—for that instant of pleasure—is all that matters. If you get pleasure from eating, drinking, and being merry, then do it—don't worry about the consequences of your actions. If you feel like getting strung out on drugs or having sex with anyone and everyone, who cares? Everything is equally absurd and equally meaningless, and it is an equal option.

This is the reason for the great increase in violence and sadism in our society—meaningless violence in a meaningless world. This kind of behavior is based on the presuppositions that are being taught to our students consciously and unconsciously year after year. Most parents figure it's just part of getting an education until one day their college senior puts a pistol to his head and blows his brains out.

I might remind you that the increase in the number of suicides among youth is astonishing. Never before have so many young people been taking their lives. Why? It is because of the godless world and life view they have been absorbing for several decades in our schools.

Parents come to me in tears, saying, "We can't understand it. Johnny went to Sunday school and church almost every week of his life. But we sent him off to college, and he came back an atheist after only one year! What did we do wrong?" The answer is simple: they sent him to an atheistic school. His parents threw him into the intellectual arena of professors with impressive degrees and tremendous persuasiveness, and these guys tore his values down and ripped his insides out.

"But," the parents argue, "we had to send him to a prestigious college so he could get a high-paying job and be successful after graduation." Are money and prestige more important than the eternal destination and soul of your child? If you throw him to the wolves, don't expect him to come back with his childhood values in tact.

Powerful Change Agents

Is this method of controlling the minds of your children simply the price paid for intellectual pursuit? Or is it an organized movement on the part of many liberal-thinking educators? I believe there is a growing counter-movement dedicated to undoing everything that we are attempting to teach our children at home and at church. These "change agents" (as they like to call themselves) have infiltrated our public school system and are committed to the destruction of all traditional moral values.

Their goal is to draw more and more power away from parents and local school boards and place it in the hands of Washington bureaucrats and the National Education Association—a left-wing group committed to the very antithesis of almost everything you and I believe. Using clever techniques, they have successfully dropped a veil over what they have done and are doing. Let me try to rip away a part of that veil, so you as parents can see the minefield into which you are ushering your children each morning. While it is true that not all public schools are bad, the National Education Association is doing everything in its power to bring all teachers and principals under its control.

The National Commission on Excellence advocates that parents should become involved in every aspect of their children's education. But the National Education Association, the union of teachers, do not want parental involvement. *NEA Today* (their official magazine) complained how one state education association fought unsuccessfully to keep its state legislature from increasing the proportion of lay citizens on the state textbook committee. NEA does not want parents to help select textbooks or even know what is in them. The material your children read and study is determined mainly by professional educators who share moral views diametrically opposite to the values of most people in our nation.

123

Whenever parents try to oppose a certain textbook, educators rise up in indignation and cry, "Censorship!" But what about the thousands of inspirational books written by well-known patriotic and Christian leaders that are excluded from your child's school library and reading list? That exclusion, when done by professional educators, is called "academic freedom." But when parents say they want a particularly obscene, profane, and godless book removed, it is called "censorship."

Most parents do not realize that the National Education Association is the most powerful political lobbying group in America today. This "progressive political movement" considers all who oppose them as "reactionaries, dangerous witch hunters, energized super-patriots, wayward dogma peddlers," according to Terry Herndon, former executive director of the NEA.

One of our nation's leading humanist educators said that maybe Johnny can't read, but at least he is compelled to go to school for twelve years and be divested of all religious superstition. What is that religious superstition? It is what you and I believe: that God is the Creator of man and the universe; that the Bible is God's Word; and that Jesus Christ is the Son of God. Some educators see the purpose of education as the eradication of this kind of thinking from your child's mind.

Why Johnny Can't Read

A *Washington Post* Poll indicated that people have less faith in the public education system in America than they do in either of the most maligned institutions in this country—the military and big banks.

Jacques Barzun, a well-known author, said in *Teachers in America:* "The once-proud and efficient public school system of the United States, especially its unique free high school for all, has turned into a wasteland where violence and vice share the time of ignorance and idleness."

Recently I talked to a man from a church I had pastored more than 20 years ago. Soon after he was saved he started serving the Lord. He witnessed to people and became active in the calling program of the church. In those days he had a very quick temper. Time and again he confessed with tears that he had treated somebody rudely or gotten angry when he shouldn't have. In spite of his flaws, however, I could see continual growth. Today he is gentle and self-controlled. The remarkable change from what he once was could be seen by fellow members at a meeting where he was falsely accused by a hostile man who based his remarks on hearsay. A few years ago my friend would have unleashed a tirade of angry words. But on this occasion his reaction was quiet and Christlike. Hearing this rejoiced...

words. Are they justified? According to ... teachers were physically assaulted by ...lic schools in one year! Drug use and ... in the schools has increased along with ...uity, lack of discipline, vandalism, rape, ...de. Sounds like a wasteland to me. ...mics? When American students were ...ents from other major technologically ...ur students did not score first or even ... nineteen subjects tested. In fact, they ...n of them. The national average on ...ores and Scholastic Aptitude Tests has ...ly in recent years. We all know that ...ut how many realize that Johnny can't ... for himself? ...llions of dollars on education in this ...y rate has increased five times. Colum-...rote that if Boeing-Aircraft doubled its ... funding from the Federal government, ... to produce an airplane that could fly higher, faster, or farther than the antiquated B-52, would that be an argument for additional funding? The NEA says, "Yes. What we need is more money."

Other experts conclude that money may not be the solution; it may be the problem. They point out that private schools, where teachers make far less money and operate on lower budgets, consistently turn out a far superior product. One teacher in a private religious school took the standard test, which 20 percent of the public school teachers in his city had failed, and gave it to his eighth grade class. One hundred percent of the eighth graders passed the test.

Who's Clarifying What?

If children aren't being taught to read and write, what are they being taught? Ask your children. Make yourself aware of the subject matter and content of the textbooks they use in the classroom. Of course, this may not be easy since some textbooks are not allowed to be taken out of the classroom. In some cases, it has taken congressmen, senators, and even the courts, to give parents the right to read some of the books or see some of the films being shown to their children in public schools.

One of the goals of public school educators is to help students clarify their values—without the aid of any absolutes or Biblical teaching, of course. This process, called "values clarification," uses methods like the magic circle, sensitivity training, psycho-social games, and dramas to shape your child's values.

Survival games are played in which children must decide who can live and who must die. You know, the old "lifeboat" story with six people in the boat and only five can live. It is interesting to note that the clergyman is usually the oldest, most expendable person mentioned. Which of the six should be thrown overboard? Sometimes a film shows a screaming person being bodily tossed into the sea. Sound like something you'd like your children to see?

What about the field trips your children take? Are you aware of the places they are going? In one state, fifth grade students were taken to a mortuary to view the embalming room. When they returned to the classroom, their assignment was to fashion a coffin for themselves from a shoebox. Other students were told to list ten different methods of committing suicide and then choose the method they would use.

What is the consequence of this sort of death training? Listen to this testimony: "My sixteen-year-old son's chemistry teacher explicitly described in class how to commit suicide 'painlessly' by drowning yourself. The next night, my son tied weights to his ankles and drowned himself in the swimming pool. It certainly was not painless, as he'd been told; he tried in vain to get loose and choked to death."

Values clarification is nothing more than a blatant attempt to destroy all absolute morality and all traditional values by telling a student he can make up whatever morals and values he feels are right for him. Students are presented with several choices in a given situation and told to pick one. Which would you prefer: to discover that you are pregnant, that you have herpes, or that your parents are getting divorced? Only negative options are presented. No wonder there are no right answers. What effect do you think this kind of questioning has on children exposed to it year after year?

A fifth grader was asked, "If you were terminally ill, what would you do?" Five suggestions were given, and two of them involved mercy killing. An elementary class was presented with this situation: A twelve-year-old girl is pregnant. What should she do—abort the baby or go through with the pregnancy and put the child up for adoption? The teacher told the children to stand to indicate their vote. Everyone in the class stood and voted to have the baby aborted—except one young girl who was herself adopted. How do you think she felt to discover that her classmates would prefer her to be dead rather than adopted?

Young students are asked such questions as, "At what age should you—(followed by a list of immoral activities)." After writing down their answers, they are asked, "Do you think children of such and such an age should involve themselves in. . . ." As each activity is listed, children are made to stand in a line in the middle of the classroom and told to step to the right or left depending on their answer. The peer pressure brought upon children in a situation like that is tremendous. Are your children forced into making these kinds of decisions day after day? Maybe it's time you found out.

What can you do? I have only two suggestions. One is to get involved in the public schools, find out what is going on, and do everything you possibly can to change it. I thank God for Christian parents, teachers, and principals who are working in the public schools and maintaining a strong moral and spiritual influence in spite of overwhelming opposition.

The second option parents can make involves an alternative to public education. Let's take a close look at this option in the next chapter.

Heavenly Father, You have given us our children as special gifts. It is our responsibility to care for them and to train them up in the nurture of the Lord. Help us to do that and to find for them schools where Your truth is not denied and Your gospel is not rejected. In Jesus' name. Amen.

14

TRAIN UP A CHILD

"Train up a child in the way he should go: and when he is old, he will not depart from it" (Proverbs 22:6). For centuries, Christians have taken these words very seriously, striving to bring up their children in the fear and admonition of the Lord. This is also the goal of many modern Christian parents. Because they want their children to live godly, moral lives, they teach them at home, bring them to Sunday school and church, and daily pray with and for them.

But is that enough? What effect does the six to seven hours a day spent in school have on your children? Are they attending a school that reinforces and supports the godly values you are teaching them at home? Or are they going every weekday to a school that undermines, questions, and sometimes blatantly negates all your biblical and moral instruction?

Fortunately for us as Americans, there are alternatives to a public school education. In the last ten years, thousands of Christian schools have been established across our nation. "But," you say, "what about the high cost of private education?" Your child's education is a matter of priorities. What is more important—a trip to Disney World, or your child's soul and mind? How much would a Christian parent in Russia sacrifice to avoid sending their children to a state-run school?

True And False Concepts

What is the difference between a public school education and a Christian school education? In a Christian school, education is centered in God and based on the truth of Scripture. In order for education to be effective, it must be education in truth. If a child is learning falsehood, he is not learning anything valuable at all.

Secular education centers around the false concept that God does not exist. The result is that reality is ripped away from its source. When students try to absorb this false sense of reality, their thinking becomes confused, and chaos results. Because all absolutes have been denied, there is no basis for morality, making secular education basically amoral. How can a teacher take a position on morals when he doesn't have a foundation for them or the system forbids it?

The basic assumptions of *who man is* and *how he came into being* determine how children are viewed by teachers. If secular educators have a false view of the nature of their students, how can they teach them properly? Teachers who see their students as having evolved from the slime approach them as animals in need of training like a rat or a monkey. This materialistic view of children has another false assumption: that man is basically good with natural inborn urges that must not be stifled but allowed full expression—no matter what the consequences.

Education, to the secular educator, is basically a life-adjusting process—not so much a matter of learning. That sounds reasonable, but how can someone with a materialistic viewpoint that centers around selfish goals teach children to adjust realistically to life? The real reason man has so much trouble adjusting to life is never mentioned. Man's *sin* is never acknowledged or dealt with because secular education has no answer for it.

In secular education, students are taught that "man can do it on his own; Christianity is only a crutch for the weak." Children are forced to adjust to life in a world without

Christ—without God—and they just cannot do it. No wonder our young people fall apart and turn to drugs and alcohol when the pressures become unbearable.

Christian teachers believe that man was created in God's image but that this image was marred by sin. God's Word teaches that man, whose mind is filled with confusion, is a fallen creature, distorted and disoriented by sin. Fallen man is at war with himself, and he needs to be made whole. Part of the Christian education process is to integrate the personality into wholeness.

Wholeness comes from being made right with God through Jesus Christ. The goal of Christian education is to make the child aware of his sin, instruct him in God's forgiveness through Jesus Christ, and channel the child's natural urges into wholesome expression that will bring glory to his Creator. When a child is reconciled to God, his identity as a person becomes clear to him. In addition, he can be taught how to be reconciled to others and have wholesome relationships. That is how a child learns to adjust to both his environment and the world in which he lives.

Each year many of the children in our Christian school here at Coral Ridge come to know Jesus Christ personally as their Savior. Once they have experienced salvation, they are set on a course of wholeness, right relationships, and abundant living. What better start can a child have for the life-adjusting process?

Striving For Excellence

In addition to the foundation of spiritual truth, Christian education strives for *academic excellence*. Anything that bears the name of Christ should be excellent. At Westminster Academy here at Coral Ridge, more than 60 percent of the teachers have master's degrees or beyond. Many of our first grade students end the year reading at third and fourth grade levels.

During the first year of our academy, about half of our students came from other Christian and private schools. The other half came from the public school system. An interesting dichotomy soon appeared. About half the students were making A's and B's on their report cards, and the other half were getting D's and F's. Only a few students were receiving C's. After studying this phenomenon, we discovered a strong correlation between the grades students were making and the kind of school they had previously attended. The children who had studied in Christian and private schools had mastered learning skills far superior to those who had attended public schools.

The academic emphasis of the public school system continues to decline as a result of a godless philosophy that teaches false concepts of education and discipline. How can children learn anything in the atmosphere of chaos and confusion that exists in some classrooms? Students have no respect for their teachers or principals because they have never been taught to submit to those in authority over them.

The permissiveness of the last two decades has produced lawlessness in our society today. This state of lawlessness in some classrooms has grown out of a parental and educational attitude that believes Johnny is basically a good boy who simply expresses his individuality by shouting, biting, hitting, and swearing. In fact, some parents make it clear that they do not want their children disciplined by the teacher at school.

God's Word calls us to discipline. As disciples of Jesus Christ, we are taught to deny ourselves, exercise self-control, and not give in to anger, lust, or pride. The guidelines for Christian behavior are clearly spelled out in the Bible, and these are taught to children in Christian schools. Kids need boundaries. Without them they feel insecure, unstable, and unloved. Although children may rebel against rules and regulations, they actually feel more secure when they know what the perimeters are.

One of the goals of Christian education is to teach children self-discipline by the renewing of their minds with God's Word. They are not just told to "be good," but children are taught how to behave and conduct themselves in a manner that is pleasing and glorifying to God.

You Are What You Believe

Another fundamental element of Christian education that most secular schools omit is a balanced emphasis on *patriotism*. Although our nation has many flaws and imperfections, it is still the most blessed nation that has ever existed in human history. We enjoy more freedom, more opportunities, and more abundance than any other country in the world—both past and present. Most secular educators fail to realize that America's blessings are a direct result of our nation's strong Christian and biblical foundations and that many social problems can be traced to a departure from those foundations.

Why has America been so blessed? You can read the twenty-eighth chapter of Deuteronomy and discover God's guidelines for a successful and prosperous country. You will also find the formula for producing a poor, unproductive, underdeveloped nation that is characterized by famine, crop failures, and disease. Look at India, a nation that has been stagnated in its poverty for several milleniums. Why? Because of what it believes. The Hindu religion teaches through pantheism that there is no reality; the external, visible world is unreal. Therefore, you do not try to correct an unreal world—you try to escape from it. Consequently, all ambition and progress die.

What about North Africa, which for centuries has been sunk in the mire of famine, superstition, and ignorance? The fatalism of Islam has kept people in bondage. They believe that man's life is predetermined by Allah, who has fated it; human initiative cannot change fate or accomplish anything of significance. The result is perpetual stagnation.

Many nations in the East follow Buddhism, which teaches that life is irreparably evil and cannot be changed. Man's only hope is to rid himself of all desire for any improvement in this life. The goal is not a more abundant life but extinction. This kind of thinking severs the roots of social advancement.

Do you see why what we believe determines what we will become and how we will live our lives? Do you want your children to be exposed day after day to the atheistic, humanistic beliefs of secular educators? If not, maybe it's time to consider the alternatives of Christian education.

Gambling With Eternity

Are all public schools bad? No. Some are still doing a good job educationally. Their standards are high, and their teachers are excellent. Aren't there many godly teachers and principals working in our public schools? Yes, but their hands are tied and their mouths are shut by the Supreme Court.

With a few precautions, you can send your child to public school. *If* your child receives a sound, biblical education at church and Sunday school; *if* you as his parents are balancing out the false concepts presented in public school with strong and wise counsel; *if* your child is bold, courageous, and not afraid of persecution by students and teachers—then he may survive twelve years of peer pressure, humanistic brainwashing, and godless indoctrination.

"Well," you may say, "I've sent my children to public school, and it hasn't hurt them yet." May I remind you that you are gambling with the eternal soul of your child? Why take a chance if an alternative is available to you? And if there is no good Christian school in your area, then look for other alternatives and be absolutely sure that the three critical *ifs* I mentioned are in effect in your child's life. When eternity is at stake, I want all the odds in my favor.

A family living in Colorado gambled and almost lost. When they moved to a larger, more expensive home, they were too far away for their children to continue attending a Christian school. Although the parents were concerned, they felt that the children had received a good foundation both academically and spiritually. "We can't protect them forever," they said. "Maybe it's time they learned to contend with the real world."

The son went to the local junior high school and was able to withstand most of the peer pressure that faced him day after day. Their daughter, however, who entered sixth grade in the neighborhood elementary school, was not as strong. Her values from that time on were molded by friends whose influence led her into smoking, shoplifting, drinking, and drugs. The precious Christian parents who were leaders in their church went through untold agony and humiliation over their daughter's delinquent behavior and subsequent arrest. Although she finally reformed her ways, this daughter still has not yielded her heart to the Lord.

The evidence is overwhelming—the vast majority of students who are turned out of Sunday school and into the secular high schools and colleges are overcome by the unbelief, immorality, and ungodliness that prevails. "Train up a child in the way he should go, and when he is old he will not depart from it." It is your responsibility, Christian parent, to see that your child receives the proper training in truth and holiness. If he does not, then don't be surprised when he departs from "the way he should go." If he is properly trained, then expect God to fulfill His promise and keep your child on the right track.

Father, may we as parents take seriously Your admonition that our children should be taught what is true—in church, at home, and in school. May they not depart from the way they should go because we have taught them that Jesus Christ is the Way, the Truth, and the Life. May they grow up to bring glory to Your name. Amen.

15

SEX EDUCATION

I recently heard a television panel discuss sexual problems in our society. Several experts were being interviewed, and the question was asked, "Are there no moral standards anymore concerning sex?" One of the experts replied, "No." His answer was accepted, without question. They all concluded that the mores have gone by the board, and we live in a new, free society where anything goes.

Americans are in the midst of a tremendous revolution— a sexual revolution. Never in all recorded history has there been such a complete and rapid change in the sexual mores of any society as we have seen in this generation.

Some Christian parents prefer to take a "see-no-evil, hear-no-evil, speak-no-evil" approach, hoping this revolution will not invade their little family kingdom. Sex education within the family framework is absolutely essential because your children are going to become educated about sex one way or another. A teen pregnancy rate shows that 40 percent of today's fourteen-year-old girls will be pregnant at least once by the age of twenty.

Havelock Ellis, one of the pioneers in this field, said that to forbid proper sex education to children is like refusing them a drink of pure water just because there are plenty of mud puddles in the street. If we, as Christian parents, don't give them what they need, our young people will drink the dirty, stagnant filth of the world. One young lady said she learned many things about sex when she was growing up, but one thing she never learned was that it was enjoyable. What a tragedy.

On the other hand, to allow the public schools to educate your children about this precious God-given privilege is an equal tragedy. There has been great turmoil in our country in the last ten years about the matter of sex education in public schools. Is it good, or is it bad? I, for one, am opposed to it. Some people would say, "Why, that's very narrow-minded. Do you want to keep our children in ignorance?" Not at all! It is not the *facts* of sexuality that I am concerned about being taught but rather the interpretation of the facts.

What Is Being Taught?

Sex education in the public schools is taught from a humanistic viewpoint. This materialistic, atheistic, amoral—or immoral—world view sees man as nothing more than a complicated animal. Consequently, sex is considered one of man's natural appetites, like that of the animals. Therefore, it is healthy to indulge this sexual appetite when it gets hungry, regardless of the time or the circumstances. They say that to inhibit its indulgence can lead to all manner of psychological disruption in the interior being of the person.

Our young people are told that if they do not have sex as teenagers, there is obviously something wrong with them. The media promotes the idea that a young person who lives a chaste life will be so overcome with sexual frustration that they will have a nervous breakdown. The facts indicate, however, that our mental institutions are filled with people who are overwhelmed by their guilt because they have flaunted the laws of God in this realm.

What would you think about a man who never kissed his wife until they were engaged? Would he be less well-adjusted than the unmarried woman who told me she had had frequent sexual relations with many men? Comparing these

138

two lifestyles, you would expect, from what we hear today, that the man would be a frustrated lunatic and the woman a liberated, healthy female enjoying life to the fullest. Such is not the case, however. The man who never kissed his wife until they were engaged is Billy Graham. The woman I mentioned is confined to the mental ward of a local hospital where she is overwhelmed with guilt and completely broken in her psyche.

No, it is not the facts of sex that I am concerned about, but the idea that it is simply a materialistic urge to be satisfied, regardless of whether it is in marriage or outside of marriage. Extramarital relationships are considered all right if the persons involved are sincere or in love. Sex is considered wrong only when it is forced or when it violates the other person's "rights."

Sexual promiscuity is encouraged from puberty to senility. If teenagers want to fool around, that's easily solved by giving thirteen-year-olds contraceptives. When that doesn't work, there is always the alternative of abortion. Students are encouraged to go to Planned Parenthood for all of their needs—both contraceptive and abortive.

Public school sex education courses teach children that there is *no* absolute standard by which to determine whether or not they should have sex with someone else if they have an inclination to do so. Neither are they taught with what kind of partner to have sex. One manual used in a high school health class taught that there are only two qualifications for joining in any kind of sexual activity: that an individual feels it is right for him or her at that particular time with that particular person; and that he or she is fully able to handle the sex, the love, and the consequences.

But the *consequences* are seldom spelled out. Any psychologist will tell you that sexual expression outside of wedlock produces the profoundest disappointments, the most tragic interpersonal relationships, and the grossest ugliness known to man. Studies show that promiscuous girls in their teens have a five to one greater incidence of cervical cancer. Is that fact presented by the secular humanists who write the teaching manuals for our schools?

This kind of immoral or amoral teaching is destroying our young people. That is why I am opposed to sex education in the public schools. I believe our children need to be taught what the Bible says about sex.

Who Sets The Standards?

When I heard the "experts" say there are no absolutes concerning sex, my heart cried out, "What about God? What about the ten commandments? Does the One who created us not have the right to govern us?" The moral standards were given by the Creator of this universe, the Maker of man. Yet by ignoring these standards, man places himself in eternal peril.

If God, the ruler of the universe, created man out of the dust of the ground, then He certainly has a right to determine what is best for us. But, on the other hand, if we accidentally and spontaneously emerged out of some primeval slime—if we clawed our way out of the jungle— then no one can tell us what to do. We are autonomous man; we are god unto ourselves.

That is precisely why unbelieving humanists fight so passionately to have evolution taught in public schools; and why they fight so vehemently to have the teaching of creationism eliminated from textbooks. They mock, ridicule, and oppose biblical creationism because it teaches that there is a Creator. If there *is* a Creator, then there is Someone to whom we must and will give an account of our lives.

Many young and older people have thrown off all thought of God's constraint and completely rebelled against their Creator and Lawgiver. "No one can tell me what to do. It's my body, and I'll do as I please." "If it feels good, do it!" Isn't that the moral principle by which many people are living in our hedonistic society—a society that has made pleasure its greatest goal?

Many parents themselves engage in some of the so-called lesser forms of sexual immorality—the suggestive look or the unclean thought. Yet Jesus specifically taught that looking lustfully on a member of the opposite sex is the same as committing adultery. (See Matthew 5:28.) Your kids know what you watch on television after they go to bed. They see the way you look at the girls on the beach. You're not fooling anyone.

The devil would have us believe that God wants to keep us from experiencing a fulfilled and happy life. Satan is still promoting the same lie that he whispered to Eve in the garden: "Don't listen to God. He's not with it! His view is narrow and close-minded. He only wants you to be miserable and frustrated. If you really want to get the most out of life, do things *my* way."

Our loving heavenly Father knows the best way for us to live. By following God's laws and living as a disciple of Jesus Christ, our lives will be as blessed as they can be in this sin-cursed world. God is on our side, and He wants what is best for us.

Even many Christians have a mistaken idea of God's best for us. They think *happiness* is the goal for which we should strive. But God's best for us is *holiness*. Most people cringe at the mention of the word "holiness." To them it sounds legalistic and, for all practical purposes, impossible. But a holy life is possible with the help of the Holy Spirit dwelling within us.

We are creatures of habit. Every time we yield to a certain temptation, the weaker we become in that area of our lives. But every time we resist that temptation, we become stronger and stronger. With God's help, we can overcome temptation because "greater is he that is in you, than he that is in the world" (1 John 4:4). When pleasing Him becomes more important than satisfying ourselves, we will strive to bring every thought, every look, and every act into conformity to Him who is holy and who made us for Himself.

People who seek only happiness seldom, if ever, find it. But if holiness is our goal, then we will find the happiness others are vainly searching for—along with the by-products of joy, peace, and contentment.

That is the message you need to convey to your young people before they are deceived by the lies of humanistic sex education. If your children learn this truth at an early age, you will spare them years of anxiety, discontent, and selfish living. Teach your children that God loves them and wants only the best for them. Help them understand that all His commandments, laws, and instructions are for their own good—to keep them out of trouble so they can enjoy life to the fullest.

Tomb, Tavern, Or Temple?

During the Victorian era, many people adopted the ancient pagan philosophy of the Platonists who considered the body evil and basically a *tomb* for the soul. All sexual functions were looked upon as evil and a source of embarrassment and confusion. Today, people have gone to the other extreme, and the body is seen not as a tomb but as a *tavern* to be used for pleasure. The Bible presents the body as neither tomb nor tavern but as a *temple* of the Holy Spirit.

As Christian parents, we must settle in our own hearts what we believe about the purpose of sex before we can begin to instruct our children. It's easy to adopt the world's view that says free sex is *not* immoral but healthy. It takes a knowledgeable and informed parent to be able to sift through all the garbage being thrown at our children today. Sexual temptation is all around us—books, movies, television, pornography. You can't even pick up a news magazine or watch television without being bombarded by commercials depicting some sexually suggestive scene.

Fornication has become a way of life. I have talked to many young people who did not know there was anything wrong with two unmarried people having sex. No one had ever explained the seriousness of such actions before marriage. But the Bible makes it clear that the consequences can be eternal: "Neither the sexually immoral nor idolaters nor adulterers, nor male prostitutes nor homosexual offenders . . . will inherit the kingdom of God" (1 Corinthians 6:10, *NIV*).

It is often said that premarital sex is the key to a successful marriage. "If you don't try on the suit, how will you know it fits? Who buys a new car without first taking it for a spin?" Sounds more like a trumped-up excuse to me. The Kinsey Report says that the majority of couples whose marriages flounder had pre-marital sexual experience.

The question is often asked, "Doesn't love make it all right? If I really love him or her, it is okay, isn't it?" But then I have to ask, "Doesn't true love involve total concern for the well-being of the other person? Isn't true love a permanent caring for all facets of the personality, life, and health of another person? How can such love exist outside of marriage?"

I would ask two young people who say they are in love and want to have sex: "Do you love each other enough to forego what might be a meaningful, but momentary, experience of sexual union for the sake of creating the best conditions for sexual and marital happiness in the future?" Those who wait to consummate their love after marriage answer "yes" to that question. True love, rather than demanding premarital sex, demands premarital chastity in order to safeguard love's highest and deepest possibilities.

Don't let your young people be deceived. Not everybody is "doing it," as they may think. There are many Christian teenagers who have made a firm decision not to have sex before marriage.

A young man wrote to his fiancee during their summer vacation from college: "You know, darling, we will have to be very careful when we get back to school next September, so we can save ourselves for our wedding night. What prevents me from asking you for or engaging in intercourse?

It is love and respect for you and the belief that a greater harmony for both of us will come when we restrict our sex relations to each other after we marry. Good night, darling. I will never love anyone more except God."

Your Child's Sexuality

The sexual revolution extends beyond the boy/girl realm and concludes that any kind of sexual relationship is all right—whether it is heterosexual or homosexual. "Gays" are becoming more accepted by society, and their lifestyle is being promoted as normal and healthy. But is it?

The concensus of psychologists and psychiatrists who have dealt with these people is that this term is extraordinarily ill chosen. If there is anything a homosexual is not, it is *gay*. Many psychiatrists have testified that these people feel trapped, condemned by society, rejected by God, and unfulfilled in life; they even hate themselves. Yet often they are incapable of doing anything about their situation, so they desperately try to justify their lifestyle to society.

Dr. Stuart Barton Babbage stated: "Homosexuals often like to believe that their homosexuality is inborn; therefore, irremediable. Such was the theory propounded approximately a century ago. It is still widely held by the uninformed and the misinformed." Today the concept of homosexuality as constitutional (in the sense of genes and chromosomes) in its origin is considered obsolete by leading scientific investigators. Most psychiatrists regard the disorder as the result of psychological rather than physical disturbances, and, consequently, it is remediable.

What are the psychologically contributing factors? Dr. Clyde Narramore, a world famous psychologist, says the personality factor that leads to homosexuality can occur subtly in childhood. In fact, many homosexuals cannot recall a time when they felt any differently about their sex. This, of course, leads to the erroneous conclusion that they were born that way.

A child first loves himself. Then he learns to love his parents. Next, a child learns to love others of the same sex. Where do most boys from the ages of eight to twelve spend their spare time? Playing Little League, going to Cub Scouts, and doing things with the "guys." Ask the average ten-year-old boy his opinion of girls, and he will probably grimace and say, "Yuck!"

The next stage of development comes when a young person is attracted to the opposite sex and begins to have feelings of affection for them. When a child does not move on to this stage, it is probably because something arrested his normal personality development. The result is that he fails to progress into normal heterosexual love but rather gets stuck at the third stage—love for others of the same sex.

What is the cause of this arresting? Dr. W. L. Carrington, in his book, *Psychology, Religion and Human Needs,* says that the main cause is abnormal relationships with adults that interfere with the normal growth to maturity. This does not necessarily mean sexual relationships, but any kind of abnormal relationships with adults. The most common of these is the over-persistent attachment of a boy to his over-possessive mother.

Dr. Narramore points out that it is widely agreed that this personality disorder largely results from two major contributing factors in childhood. One factor is a mother who dominates the home, her husband, and the children. The second cause is a weak father who does not set an example of masculinity and manhood before his son. There are other causes, but these two are primary.

In a study of 106 male homosexuals in comparison with 106 non-homosexual men, researchers found several reoccuring factors. The male homosexual frequently was the mother's favorite child. She demanded to be the center of her son's attention, spending a greater than average amount of time with her son. In addition, the study found that the mother discouraged masculine activities and attitudes while encouraging feminine ones. She often used the son as an ally against her husband, often preferred her son to her husband's company, and was unduly concerned about protecting the child from physical injury.

On the other hand, the father was usually weak or absent from the home and failed to encourage masculine attitudes. The homosexual generally experienced a poor father/son relationship and was his father's least favored child. This lack of acceptance by the father caused the child to have feelings of both hatred and fear toward him. The homosexual often had little respect for his father and did not feel accepted by him. The father, in turn, did not express affection for his son.

I have included this information to show the impact parents can have on the personality and sexual development of their child. Fathers and mothers must realize and fulfill their God-ordained roles as husbands and wives. The future and eternity of your child may be at stake.

Sex Education At Home

You can teach your children at home—in your family devotions—about the proper purpose of sex. A simple and practical study centered on God's Word will help you lay the foundation for your children. In the first lesson, study what God's Word has to say about purity, chastity, and holiness. Next, look at the Bible's teaching on immorality, lust, sexual sin, and the consequences of such actions.

Once your children know that sex was created solely for the pleasure and purpose of marriage, the boundaries will be established. Then they will be able to compare and analyze anything they learn from any other source with the scriptural knowledge you have taught them. Encourage your children to come to you with any questions or teaching that contradicts the Bible and your instructions.

Educating your children in the area of proper sexual behavior is not as difficult as you think. In fact, most of your teaching will come as you sit watching television together or discussing the day's events. That is your opportunity to say, "That kind of thinking is wrong. God's Word says. . . ." Or, "What do you think would be the consequences of that kind of behavior?" Stay alert to every situation—you can bet your children know exactly what is going on!

Avoid trying to scare your children into sexual purity. It may have the opposite effect and create rebellion against God's Word. Or they may grow up thinking sex is dirty and something to be avoided. Balanced teaching in this area is of utmost importance. Once your children know God's view of sex and marriage, you must teach them that only love and devotion to Jesus Christ will keep them living holy lives. The motivation for sexual purity must come from a desire to please God and walk in obedience to Him.

Heavenly Father, help us as parents to realize the responsibility we have to lead holy lives before You and before our children. Cleanse us from all secret and hidden sins. By the power of Your Holy Spirit, give us the grace and strength to resist temptation. Father, we need Your wisdom to help us teach our children what Your Word says about sex and marriage. We look to You to be our guide. In Jesus' name. Amen.

Part Three

LEARNING TO LIVE
AS A FAMILY

16

WHEN YOU SIT AT HOME

"The most vivid and meaningful memories in all of my youth," said one elderly gentleman, "were the memories of those many hours when my father and mother after dinner would gather the family together in the living room, and my saintly dad would take down the old Bible and read a passage, or else pass it to one of us children. The Word of God would be read and discussed. Happily we would sing praise to God around the piano and then kneel together in prayer. I can still hear my mother's voice and my father praying for me by name. These are memories which I can never forget—memories that have altered my whole life: formed it, trained it, guided it, developed it—memories which I consider the greatest heritage that my parents could possibly have given me."

After he and the other five children had left home and gone their separate ways, this man said, "I knew that still each night when my mother and father gathered together by themselves with the Lord in the living room and on their knees, they would be remembering me in prayer."

What an inheritance to leave to a child! Four of these children went into the ministry, and the other two became active laymen who served Christ faithfully. What will your children be doing with their lives after they have left home and gone their separate ways?

Praying Parents

Family worship is one of the most lasting and effectual tools for training children in the nurture and admonition of the Lord. Sad to say, despite the fantastic results which it has had in past generations, family devotions is today one of the most neglected of the Christian disciplines.

Andrew Murray, author of the classic works, *With Christ In The School Of Prayer* and *The Ministry Of Intercession,* also had praying parents. They not only had regular family devotions, but they interceded daily for each of their eleven children. In addition, Murray's father spent every Friday evening praying for worldwide revival. Andrew vividly remembered standing outside the study door listening to his father crying out to God and pleading for an outpouring of the Holy Spirit. Little did Andrew know that later he would be instrumental in being part of the answer to his father's prayers.

Mrs. Murray's life was characterized by the peace, contentment, and joy she shared with her household. How did she achieve such peace of mind while caring for such a large family? Her secret was private times of communion with God. When her bedroom door was shut, children and servants knew that mother must not be disturbed. Were her prayers answered? All of her eleven children either became ministers or ministers' wives, each having a tremendous impact on their nation and God's kingdom.

Parents who pray *with* and *for* their children build walls of protection around them that keep the enemy at bay and keep the children from straying out of God's will. Isn't that a small price to pay for the eternal safety of the little ones God has given you?

Parents Or Strangers?

The Bible says, "Train up a child in the way he should go." That doesn't mean you get some stranger to train your children—this verse is directed at mom and dad. Many parents bring their child to Sunday school and make that the sum total of his Christian training. But that's not what God had in mind at all.

The Old Testament makes it clear that God intended for parents to train children daily in the home.

> Hear, O Israel: The Lord our God, the Lord is one. Love the Lord your God with all your heart and with all your soul and with all your strength. These commandments that I give you today are to be upon your hearts. Impress them on your children. Talk about them *when you sit at home* and when you walk along the road, when you lie down and when you get up—Deuteronomy 6:4-7, *NIV,* italics added.

I've heard parents say, "I can't understand it! I trained him up in the way he should go. I sent him to Sunday school every week. But now he's involved in drugs, sin, and rebellion. What did I do wrong?"

Although Sunday school and church are fine supplements to Christian teaching, they are no substitute for parental training within the family. To provide substitutes is to disobey this direct command of God. Training children in the ways of God rests squarely upon the shoulders of the parents—and most explicitly upon the father. Throughout the Bible, verses concerning spiritual leadership and education of children in the home are directed toward the father.

In many families, the little bit of spiritual training children do receive is provided by the mother. This gives an effeminate and weak picture of Christianity to young boys, later causing them to turn and follow their worldly dad instead of their godly mother.

Grown children have said to me, "I never once heard my father pray." Will your children say that about you? One forty-five-year-old father decided to turn over a new leaf:

"My children have never heard me pray. But if God is gracious enough to give me one more day, that situation is going to be changed."

A woman once told me, "When I was a child, we didn't have family devotions in our home, but I had a friend in the neighborhood who did. I often visited her and watched as this family lifted their hearts together to God, and my soul was touched. I vowed right then that I would never marry a man who couldn't pray and lead his family in worship."

Setting The Tone

How you as parents approach family worship will set the tone and the attitude your children will take. If they hear you grumbling about missing the evening news or being pressed for time, the children will begin to complain about having to participate. Don't be a stumbling block to family worship by having a negative attitude.

Tension between family members can destroy the atmosphere of love and peace that should surround this time together. What can be more devastating to the training of a child than to see parents who are unreconciled to one another leading their families in hypocritical worship? Let this coming together be an occasion for settling differences so the love of Christ can prevail. Jesus said, "If you are offering your gift at the altar and there remember that your brother has something against you, leave your gift there in front of the altar. First go and be reconciled to your brother; then come and offer your gift" (Matthew 5:23-24, *NIV*).

Your children need to hear you pray, "Father, forgive me, I was wrong." When they realize that parents make mistakes and seek God's forgiveness as well as that of the other person, they will learn to do the same. Children can spot a phony a mile away. They know when you're being honest and when you're covering up. The last thing you want to teach your child to be is a hypocrite.

How To Have Family Devotions

The first step in having regular family devotions is to *set a definite time and stick to it.* Leaving the time open-ended probably means it will never happen; other things will invariably demand your attention. A time of worship together every day brings the greatest longtime results, but if you can only manage to get together three times a week that is still better than not at all. Choose a time when everyone in the family is generally present. It may be in the morning before the kids leave for school, as long as it's not too rushed.

Most families at least try to sit down to the evening meal together. But don't combine eating with devotions—especially before the meal. You don't want your children to associate praying with cold food. Sitting around a table of dirty dishes after the meal doesn't create a worshipful atmosphere either. Moving to another, more comfortable room signals to the children that this is a special time for the family.

Try to involve every member of the family. The format should be geared so there is something meaningful for every age child. If your six-year-old can read, let him read the Bible passage for the day. If your twelve-year-old can play the guitar or the piano, have him accompany the singing.

Keep your format from becoming too structured. Read the Word of God and have some explanatory comments about it; have a time of prayer; sing a song. At other times, you may spend the entire time in prayer, singing, or meditating upon the words of the great hymns.

Use additional materials and teaching tools. There are many excellent aids for family devotions published by Christian companies. Go to your local bookstore and look for devotional books geared to the ages of your children. Make sure each child has a version of the Bible he can read and understand. Songbooks and hymnals are wonderful sources of doctrine and inspiration. Memorizing Scripture choruses is an easy way to remember Bible verses.

Keep it simple. Don't bore your children with long, drawn-out sermons. Let their daily experiences be the guideline for the topics you discuss. Study areas that are relevant to your family life, dealing with the problems you face each day in the home. Find out what the Bible has to say about criticism, complaining, disobedience, lying, anger, etc. Or maybe you need to emphasize what God's Word has to say about building the qualities of truth, integrity, purity, and honesty. This will take some planning on your part as a parent, but you will be molding and training your child in a way no one else can.

Prayer should be an important part of your family worship time. When your children see God answer the specific requests made during your times of worship, prayer will soon become an integral part of their daily lives. If their cat is sick, the children learn that God cares. If they are having trouble in school, they know God will help them.

The greatest truth your children can ever learn is that God loves them. When they know they have a loving heavenly Father who cares for them, protects them, provides for them, and is concerned about their every need, your children will not be swayed by the world's philosophies. The best way to teach your children about God's love is through prayer.

Present the plan of salvation. One of the greatest thrills a parent can have is leading his own children to a saving knowledge of Jesus Christ. Explain the plan of salvation over and over again using a different approach until you feel every child really understands who Jesus is, why He died for them, and how they can receive him as personal Savior. What better gift can you give your child than eternal salvation and the security of knowing his sins are forgiven? That's the key to making sure your child does not depart from the way.

A Matter Of Conviction

Most parents are convinced that certain things are essential to the well-being of their children—like eating three meals a day and brushing their teeth. Despite a busy schedule and the pressures of daily living, we still manage every day to find time to feed our children three meals because we know it is important to their health. We make sure they get foods from all four food groups and encourage them to drink their milk.

Then after we feed them, we ask, "Did you brush your teeth?" How many times have you said that to a child proceeding hastily out the back door? We lecture our children on the importance of dental hygiene and what will happen if they don't brush. So our boys and girls brush up and down, over and over, day after day.

If parents think that something is vital, they will see that it gets done. Parents make sure their children receive medical attention and see that they go to school and take music lessons. And all these things are important. But many parents fail to realize that their most important responsibility is to see that their children are trained in the ways of God.

What difference will it make to have healthy, talented children with sparkling teeth and educated minds who have turned their back on God and are living for the world, the flesh, and the devil? Our children are God's gifts to us to raise and train while they are on earth. How will God rate our job as parents if our children end up in hell?

Maybe the problem is that it takes longer for cavities to develop in the soul than on the teeth. When we can't see our child's inner man shriveling up from lack of spiritual nourishment, it's easy to neglect feeding him. If you were really convinced that daily devotions with your children are important, you would make a point to have them.

When should you start having family worship? Today. Before it is too late—before your children are gone and you are left with nothing but heartache and remorse for failing to fulfill your God-given duty. Start *right now*—before the cement of their character is fully set—while you still have an opportunity to form their lives.

Father, help us to understand that Christian homes and godly lives don't just happen, but they are built systematically and daily as Your Spirit trains and molds our souls into the image of Jesus Christ. Lord, help us to seek Your face together each day in our homes and teach Your Word to our children when we rise up and when we lie down. When we sit in our homes and walk by the way, may they hear us speak of the blessings of God, the greatness of our Creator, the love of Christ, and the wonders of His grace. May we give our children a godly inheritance that will carry them throughout life and into eternity. In Jesus' name. Amen.

17

SECRET TO A HAPPY FAMILY

A happy home. Everyone wants to have one. Why, then, are so many families always arguing and shouting at one another? Do the words parents and children speak affect the degree of happiness experienced on a regular basis? The truth is: *words* can make or break a family. The way your family members talk to one another determines the quality of your homelife.

The power of words can be traced back to the beginning of creation when "God said"—He spoke—the earth, the sun, the sky, the animals, and man into being. Words have creative power. Of all the creatures on this planet, only man has been given the gift of speech. Communicating with other people is a unique gift that carries tremendous responsibility. "Death and life are in the power of the tongue" (Proverbs 18:21). No doubt about it—the words we speak and the way we say them affect the lives of others.

Any interpersonal relationship depends on communication, whether it is between friends and neighbors, parents and children, or husbands and wives. Communication is probably much more important than most of us realize.

In his epistle to the Ephesians, the apostle Paul deals at some length with interpersonal relationships: husbands and wives, parents and children, employers and employees. He precedes his instructions with a thorough discussion of the primary role of communication: "Speaking the truth in love" (Ephesians 4:15). All positive and fulfilling interpersonal relationships are based on this one command. Problems arise because speaking the truth in love is not always easy to do.

Some people pride themselves on always *speaking the truth*—no matter what the consequences. They tell it like it is, calling a spade a spade. But it is always other people's spades they are talking about. They may speak the truth, but they are about as loving as a bucketful of hydrochloric acid.

Psychologists often emphasize the need for *ventilation*. That means you let your emotions all hang out. You say whatever you feel. Encounter groups get together and ventilate their true feelings. If they are filled with wrath and indignation at someone across the room, they give him a tongue-lashing and thoroughly put him in his place. That may be a popular form of expression, but it is not biblical.

The Bible says we are to speak the truth in love. The apostle Paul goes on to say that the words coming out of our mouths should be "what is helpful for building others up according to their needs, that it may benefit those who listen . . . Get rid of all bitterness, rage and anger, brawling and slander, along with every form of malice" (Ephesians 4:29, *NIV*).

Our main concern should not be how it makes *us* feel, but how what we say makes other people feel. Jesus was "full of grace and truth" (John 1:14). We are not to speak the truth in anger; we are to speak the truth in love. Most of us go to one extreme or the other. We either don't speak the truth at all, or, if we do, we ventilate our hostile feelings on the other person. How is the truth spoken in your family?

See What I Did

A psychologist writing in a popular magazine described the difference between the way we treat guests in our home and the way we treat our children. What happens when a visitor comes to our house and spills coffee on the floor? "Oh, that's all right! Think nothing of it. It's just a little old rug . . . coffee doesn't stain. It could happen to anybody. In fact, I do it all the time myself." And we wipe it up.

But what happens when little Johnny toddles out of the kitchen with a glass of milk and—whoops! . . . all over the carpet. Does he get told that it happens to everybody all the time? No. He gets a three-part discourse on his past, present, and future character. "You do the same thing all the time! Can't you carry anything without dropping it? You clumsy idiot. How do you ever expect to grow up and be a doctor? You'll never even get through school if you can't learn to do better than that! How many times do I have to tell you not to. . . ." And on and on it goes.

Be careful how you speak to your children. You can speak words of life or death to them in one short phrase. And you can be sure they won't forget. The Bible says our words should build up others according to their needs. Everyone—especially children—needs to be encouraged, not beaten down until their self-worth is destroyed. Children cry out for attention, recognition, and acceptance by their parents.

When a baby is born, he kicks his feet, waves his arms, and cries for attention. Soon he learns to talk. His most frequently repeated words are: "Mommie, look! Daddy, look! See what I did." This infantile verbalization expresses one of the most deep-seated needs of the human heart: the need for acceptance and recognition from other human beings. Whether it is a baby crying, "Look, Mommie!" or a high school student laboring for his A's, the motivation is the same—parental acceptance.

Children need to be praised for their accomplishments, but they can easily detect the difference between a compliment and flattery. A compliment is a sincere expression of praise and admiration. When your second-grader brings home a perfect spelling paper, do you compliment him in an honest way? "Johnny, I'm so proud of you because you did the very best you could." Flattery is used as a ploy

161

when we really don't mean what we are saying: "Johnny, you're the best speller in the whole world." That's kind of pushing it, wouldn't you say? Compliments should give something that meets the specific needs of that child or individual without giving the child a false sense of pride.

Unwholesome Talk

The apostle Paul said, "Do not let any unwholesome talk come out of your mouths, but only what is helpful" (Ephesians 4:29, *NIV*). What would you consider unwholesome talk? Let's look at some forms of speech that are not only unbeneficial but damaging.

Criticizing and faultfinding do more damage than any other sin of the tongue. Psychologists have found that children who are continually criticized rarely grow up to be emotionally healthy. For some families, faultfinding is a way of life. They even consider it a virtue, not realizing that the Bible commands us not to judge one another's actions or thoughts. Yet innumerable families have been destroyed by this type of backbiting.

If you were to examine the conversation that goes on between people in many homes, you would often find them discussing the faults of someone who is not present to defend themselves. This kind of talking can become habit-forming and carry over into all other relationships. Someone wrote that backbiting is to another person what a knife is to the back. Are you a backbiter, a slanderer, or a gossip?

A father once told me he was concerned because his family would not share their problems and concerns with him. Yet many times I had heard this man backbiting against other people. Children are not stupid. Why would they share their problems with a father who is quick to judge and criticize? If he talks about other people in your presence, you begin to wonder what he is saying about you behind your back. You don't tell your secrets to a rattlesnake.

162

Parents must set the example in the home for healthy, uplifting conversation. Don't badmouth the kids down the street or your child's teacher. Be careful how you talk about others in the presence of your children. If you don't, you will probably hear your own words being repeated at the wrong time and in the wrong place: "My mommy said Mrs. Jones has false teeth."

The tone of voice you use when you talk can communicate more than your words. If you are sarcastic with your children, they will be sarcastic with you. "Thanks a lot! I really needed that!" Children learn to mimic not only the phrases you say but the tone in which you say it.

In the book of Romans, gossips and slanderers are listed in the same company as murderers, God-haters, and those who disobey their parents. Could it be that children who hear mom and dad gossiping about the neighbors and slandering the pastor learn to hate God and lose respect for their parents, resulting in rebellion and disobedience?

Your Yes And No

What about cursing and profanity? Some people think it is cute and laugh when a small child uses a swear word. Once the child realizes this gets attention, he is positively reinforced to say it again. How does God feel about swearing? Jesus said, "Do not swear at all . . . let your 'Yes' be 'Yes,' and your 'No' be 'No.' Anything beyond this comes from the evil one" (Matthew 5:34-37, *NIV*).

One of the ten commandments forbids the casual use of God's name: "You shall not misuse the name of the Lord your God, for the Lord will not hold anyone guiltless who misuses his name" (Exodus 20:7, *NIV*). The Jewish scribes who copied the Bible would stop before writing one of the names of God. When they came to the ineffable name of Yahweh—Jehovah—they put down their pen, took a bath, changed their clothes, prayed, confessed their sins, and meditated. Then they wrote the holy name of God.

Today we frequently hear God's holy name bandied about as freely as a tennis ball. Yet God has said He will not hold anyone guiltless who misuses His name. When we take God's name in vain, allow our children to do it, or listen to godless comedians profane the name of our Lord, we incur the anger and wrath of God. In Old Testament times using God's name as a curse word was punishable by death. If this sin were as rampant then as it is today, our arms would be weak from stoning people to death.

An Appreciative Heart

Now that we know what kinds of talk to avoid, let's look at the way God's Word says we should communicate. "Talk with each other much about the Lord, quoting psalms and hymns and singing sacred songs, making music in your hearts to the Lord. Always give thanks for everything to our God and Father in the name of Our Lord Jesus Christ" (Ephesians 5:19-20, *TLB*). If you and your family are sharing all the good things that God has done for you, there will be little time left for criticism, faultfinding, and unwholesome talk.

When parents set the example by expressing their appreciation to their spouse and to the children for small deeds of kindness or help, the level of commmunication in a home is raised. A heart and mouth that are filled with thanksgiving and praise to God will automatically bring forth words that bless others. Teach your children to say thank you, not only to adults but to one another. An appreciative spirit will carry over into their relationship with their heavenly Father and make them a joy and pleasure to be around.

When we took our daughter Jennifer on a tour of Washington, D.C., she got into the taxicab and said, "Thank you, Mommy and Daddy, for taking me to the Space Museum and the Lincoln Memorial and the White House. And thank you for the nice lunch." The taxi driver turned around and, staring at Jennifer in amazement, said, "In all the years I've been driving a cab, I have never before heard a child thank their parents for one thing."

The way your family talks to one another in public indicates to others the degree of love and respect you have for each other at home.

Listening With Love

Most people don't have any trouble communicating, but few of us know when to be quiet and listen. The book of Proverbs says that the person who answers a matter before he has heard it out is operating in folly and shame. (See Proverbs 18:13.) How many of us are guilty of interrupting people before they have finished their sentence? Do you do that to your children or your spouse? The Bible says we should be "swift to hear, slow to speak" (James 1:19). Most of us are much quicker to speak than we are to hear.

A book titled *The Awesome Power of the Listening Ear* discussed the transforming difference that listening can make in the lives of people. Some people will pay seventy-five dollars a half hour to a psychiatrist. And what does he do? He listens to them. Some of you husbands could save yourselves a lot of money by simply taking the time to listen to your wife when she talks to you.

There are several types of listeners. What kind are you? Are you the type who never stops what you are doing when someone is talking to you? If you are working on the car or washing the dishes, do you keep working while you talk with them? That kind of attitude says, "What you're saying may be all right, but it certainly doesn't demand my full attention."

Others may stop what they are doing with their body, but their eyes dart from one place to another as they look beyond the person talking. They keep things going with their eyes, and you know you don't have their full attention. You've probably seen this happen at a social gathering when two people are talking. While one is pouring out their heart, the other person is looking around for someone more exciting to talk to.

Some people will look at you and stop what they are doing, but they grunt instead of converse—"uh, yeah, huh, oh, ah." That's about all you get from them. It's like talking to a frog. Certainly no real communication takes place. Think about the last time your spouse or one of the children came to you and shared something that was important to them. How well did you listen?

Some of us are like automobile gas tanks. We are so full of ourselves, our own ideas, and our own plans that when others try to put anything in, they get splashed in the face. Good listeners are more like siphons. They know how to draw other people out. By showing true interest, they create an atmosphere that generates sharing and discussion. If there is going to be any give and take between two gas tanks, someone has to do the siphoning. If not, communication will stop.

When someone is talking with you—I don't mean the boss or someone you want to impress but one of your family members—do you focus your full attention on that person as you listen to them? I read about a little five-year-old girl who came into the house where the mother of eight was preparing dinner. The stove was covered with pots, and something was baking in the oven. The little girl said excitedly, "Mommy, Mommy! Look. I found a four-leaf clover!"

How do you think that mother responded? With, "Oh, that's nice, dear. Now don't bother mother." No. Instead, she glanced at the burners on the stove, turned them down a bit, knelt down, took the four-leaf clover, and said, "Oh, darling, that's so pretty. Where did you find it?" As they looked at it together, this very wise mother talked about the wonderful wisdom of God in creating this marvelous thing. Then she sat down on the floor with her daughter, and they carefully examined it.

When the father came home, he also listened with great interest about the clover. The mother suggested that it be put on the table at dinnertime so all the other children could admire it. Someone commenting on that incident said, "You know, I'd just like to cuddle up in that family." Wouldn't you?

We all feel special when someone shares their lives with us. But how many opportunities have we missed because we were too busy or too proud to listen to something we felt was trivial? Before your family will share with you, you must learn to share your life with them. Are you willing to become more vulnerable and share your problems, your hopes, and your disappointments with those you love the most?

Our family relationships are the most important ones we have in this world. The mother of eight knew that. She knew the importance of that moment when her daughter was forming an opinion about her self-worth and her place in the kingdom of God.

Lifting The Level Of Communication

Communication is to be the truth; it is to be in love; it is to be edifying; it is to be wholesome; it is to be thankful; it is to be open; and it is to be joyful. Do you have a sincere determination to see the level of communication in your home improved? It is possible to lift that level to the heights described in God's Word. But before that can happen, communication with Christ must first take place.

If you and your family have been reconciled to God in Jesus Christ, you are all one in Him and partakers of His Holy Spirit. And the fruit of the Spirit is love, joy, and peace. When Jesus Christ rules and reigns in the lives of your family members, peace will fill your hearts, and love will flow out of your mouths. Then when people come to your home, they will want to cuddle up and stay there.

Father, help us to seek Your peace in our homes. Help us to know that if love for You is there, then love for all will reign. Teach us, Lord, to be open and trusting so we can communicate the deep things of our heart. Bind us more closely to one another with those bonds that only come from communication on the highest level. In Jesus' name. Amen.

18

A CLIMATE-CONTROLLED HOME

Everyone talks about the weather, but no one ever does anything about it! Meteorologically, we can't change the weather outside, but we *can* control the weather inside—in our homes. We can control the emotional and spiritual climate within the boundaries of the house where we live. Several factors—words, deeds, and attitudes—determine the atmospheric conditions of our home.

Dr. Clyde Narramore, the famed psychologist, states in one of his books, "The most important factor for the emotional adjustment and well-being of a child is the emotional climate in his home." Whether your child becomes a well-adjusted young person or a juvenile delinquent; whether he is a shy introvert, incapable of mixing well with society, or an extrovert with a dynamic personality depends on the atmosphere in which he grows up.

The emotional climate in a home can create a miserable homosexual, a violent criminal, or a passive neurotic. It can destroy the physical health of a child and weaken him psychologically and spiritually. Or a home can be the place where children grow to be healthy and mature in body, soul, and spirit. The parents, however, have exclusive control over the thermostat and determine the family's emotional and spiritual temperature.

After years of counseling with families and visiting in homes, where some had troubles and some did not, I

atmospheric conditions at work in
gs. Let's take a look at a few of them.

London Lodge

London Lodge because the prevailing climate is cold and foggy. If you've ever been to England, you've experienced the cold London climate that chills down to the bone. You get the same feeling when you've been in this home for a while. No rosy glow from a warm, friendly fire greets you. Instead, among the dying embers, unforgiveness and resentment smolder, filling the air with tension and hostility. The chill comes from a lack of love.

Do you know a home like that? Perhaps you live in one. In these homes the parents and children go through the perfunctory motions of having a family life, yet their hearts are not in it. They are like dead people walking around. Family members approach one another stiffly, showing no spontaneity or outward demonstration of affection. Cold loveless eyes look at one another with suspicion in London Lodge. Someone called it "Mortuary Manor," where everything is neatly served by crisp, cool corpses. Woe to the child who lives in a loveless home like that. Misery and depression will follow him all the days of his life.

Psychologists have discovered that a child is not able to love—even on the most rudimentary level—unless he has been loved. Some parents decide to have a baby because they want someone who will love _them_. If the child is brought into the world to provide something that is lacking in the parent, a vicious cycle results. The parent expects something from the child that he is unable to give; the child never learns how to love because the parent cannot teach him.

Until we come to know the love of God in Jesus Christ, we will never be able to love anyone else. The Bible says, "We love because He first loved us" (1 John 4:19, _NIV_). Once we accept God's love for us as expressed in the gift of His Son, we can reach out in love to others.

Many people have accepted Christ as Savior, yet love remains absent from their homelife. Why? Because they have not yielded themselves completely to God. Some parents live with one foot in the world and both arms wrapped around self. I am convinced that the reason for so many miserable Christian homes is the lack of yielded lives. Homes that are a little bit of hell on earth are the dividend the devil pays for our infidelity and unfaithfulness to God.

Lack of love in a home makes it a joyless place. No one ever has any fun in London Lodge. Laughter seldom rings in the halls. Instead, a heavy blanket of doom and despair hangs in the air of this home, affecting everyone who lives there—especially the children.

Are you creating that kind of atmosphere in your home? Do your moods affect the rest of the family and set the tone for every activity? If you had to choose someone to live with, would you pick yourself? Do you have the kind of personality that sparks joy and enthusiasm? Or are you making your homelife a cold, dismal existence for your mate and your children?

Love is not a passive emotion. The apostle Paul says we must "follow after the way of love" (1 Corinthians 14:1, *NIV*). The verb *follow* in this verse means to pursue love in such an active, energetic way that it becomes our greatest goal in life.

How can you do that? Study what God's Word has to say about love. Then diligently pursue after its application in your home. Pray that the love of Jesus will fill your heart and overflow to your family. The God who can make all things new can change your home climate by taking the chill out of the air and warming the hearts of those who live there.

Hurricane Hollow

Another kind of home I have visited reminds me of *Hurricane Hollow*. As soon as the door opens, a blast of wind hits you in the face. Storm clouds of anger, bitterness, and strife continuously build into violent thunderheads and flashes of lightning. Angry words and high-pitched shouting generate a volatile atmosphere that can explode at any moment. Children never know what to expect. They live in fear of making a mistake because the consequences mean a rain of verbal abuse that destroys their self-image and creativity.

They say women's voices don't change, but have you ever heard a mother scolding her child when the phone rings? Talk about an instantaneous miracle! Little Johnny stares at the sweet, polite person talking on the phone and wonders if it is the same woman who was ranting and raving at him just a moment before.

Children who grow up in this kind of atmosphere come to hate their homelife. They look forward to the day when they are old enough to get out on their own. One young lady who lived in Hurricane Hollow said, "I was determined to marry the first guy who came along and asked me." And she did. She married a real loser, but she got out of her parents' house. "Anything was better than living with them," she said.

Parents wonder, "Why did Billy leave home at sixteen?" "Why did Susie get married at seventeen?" "Why didn't Johnny come home from college on weekends and holidays?" Why? Because the climate in the home was constantly charged with destructive tension that destroyed the child's hope for a peaceful and happy family life.

Midsummer's Nightmare

Have you ever spent a summer night in a house with the windows open and no screens? That's a *midsummer's nightmare!* As soon as you turn the lights out a buzzing sound starts circling your head, and you awake to find the place full of mosquitos.

In the home of the midsummer's nightmare, the people living there are always buzzing around and picking at each other. They draw blood from one another without even knowing why they do it. Everyone is slapping here and there trying to make a kill before they get stung.

Wise King Solomon wrote, "Catch for us the foxes, the little foxes, that ruin the vineyards, our vineyards that are in bloom" (Song of Songs 2:15, *NIV*). It's not the big mistakes that destroy our relationships; it's the little jabs that nibble away at the fabric of our marriage and family life.

I am continually amazed at the number of couples who criticize, correct, and belittle their spouses in front of other people. You wonder what it must be like in their homes if they behave like this in public. They don't think they are doing anything wrong, yet every critical and sarcastic remark stings like a viper and leaves scars that take years to heal. Their marriage and homelife become a nightmare, and they wake up one day wondering why there isn't any love, spontaneity, or warmth in their relationship. The little pests have done their damage.

When people ignore the instructions of God's Word not to judge one another—not to malign and criticize—they are sinning against God and each other. The Bible describes sin as folly. Sin is nothing other than stupidity—biblical ignorance. Most people either don't know what the Bible says, or they suppose that God is joking.

How many Christians, when God's Word tells them to do something, make light of it—even laugh about it? "Why, nagging is just a bad habit not a sin." *Is it?* "Kidding my wife about her weight isn't wrong; she knows I don't really mean it." *Does she?* "The kids know I'm only trying to help when I point out their mistakes." *Are you sure?*

So family members pick away at each other for years, and, when the husband runs away with another woman; when the wife has a nervous breakdown; and when the kids don't come home at night, everyone asks, "What did we do wrong?" Just about everything. For fifteen or twenty years you ignored everything God said about relationships and how to treat other people.

Don't let the "little foxes" destroy your home while it is still in bloom. We can change the climate in our homes by applying the teachings of Jesus Christ in the little things. Little by little, degree by degree, we can show love and act in kindness. Stamp out those little pests before your dream of a happy family life becomes a horrible nightmare.

Bonny Breezes

How would you like to live at "Bonny Breezes," where the sun of God's love shines and the warmth of the Holy Spirit blows softly, producing joy and peace? That would be wonderful, you say, but how can I change the climate in our home? The truth is: You cannot do it yourself. Only one Man in history did more than talk about the weather. Jesus Christ changed it. He calmed the storm with a command, and He can turn your homelife into a pleasant, peaceful place of serenity.

The parents and children living at Bonny Breezes are very affectionate with one another. They know the importance of a loving touch that expresses caring and concern. The apostle Paul encourages us to "aim for perfection . . . be of one mind, live in peace. And the God of love and peace will be with you. Greet one another with a holy kiss" (2 Corinthians 13:11-12, *NIV*). If that's how we are to treat the family of God, how much more affectionate should we be toward those with whom we live day after day?

Children learn the warmth of touching when they are babies. Their whole world revolves around being touched by mom and dad, grandma and grandpa, older brothers and sisters. Babies are encouraged to reach out and touch others. That is why young children are not satisfied to just be around those they love; they want to hold your hand, sit on your lap, stroke your face. And we love it! But what happens? As they grow older, we begin to put restrictions on their touching, and they soon learn to withdraw and withhold their affection. How sad.

You may have seen the television movie about a young boy who had a serious disease that forced him to live inside a sterile, plastic bubble. He spent his childhood and early adolescence totally isolated from the outside world. The affectionate touch of another human being was something foreign to him. When he met and fell in love with a young lady, he determined to risk all for the joy of being loved and experiencing intimate contact with another person.

Although very few people have ever had to live their lives in total isolation, millions live in an unseen, plastic bubble cut off by their own inhibitions, their inability to reach out, their fear of rejection, and their phobias about touching. The absence of affection always produces deep trauma—especially in children. Human touching is a natural need that can be fulfilled within the boundaries of proper behavior. Don't be afraid to express your love to your spouse and children by affectionate touching—a hand on the shoulder, a pat on the back, a hug when you leave, a kiss when you return. A simple arm around your child's shoulder could provide more therapy for him than years of counseling with a psychologist.

Dr. Frederick Treves, a famous London physician, found a young man with a hideous disease who was being displayed as the "elephant man" in a circus. When people saw him, they would gasp and shout obscenities at this grotesquely distorted figure. At the hospital where he was taken, the nurses fainted at the sight of him. His behavior was like a wild, hunted animal because that was how he had always been treated. One day, Sir Frederick asked a lovely lady to come and visit the "elephant man." She walked into the room, smiled at him, and shook his hand. As she touched him, he burst into tears. This poor, lonely man had never before felt the touch of a human hand or seen a smile directed toward him. That was the beginning of a tremendous transformation in this young man, who eventually became a valuable participant in society.

If more people, especially families, would reach out and touch one another in love and concern, our homes would be changed. The tender touch says, "I love you and care for you. You are special to me." In fact, the message of a touch carries greater impact than words could ever express. The bonny breezes blow in homes where love is not just spoken—it is lived and expressed by deeds and actions.

The House Of The Golden Rule

You are probably very familiar with the Golden Rule but never realized the power it has to change the climate in your home. "In everything, do to others what you would have them do to you" (Matthew 7:12, *NIV*).

The Greek term for "what you would" is actually "what you wish." Whatever you wish that others would do for you is how you are to treat them. "I wish he/she would. . . ." "I wish the children would. . . ." Whatever you say in that tone of voice and in those words is what you are outlining as your duty to them—especially in your family.

The Silver Rule—what you do *not* want done to yourself, do *not* do to others—works from a negative standpoint. The principle commanded by Jesus, however, demands a different attitude—"I must go out of my way to help others." That is quite different from saying, "I must do no harm to others." Even the ungodly man can boast of keeping the Silver Rule: "I've never hurt anyone; I've never stolen anything; I've never killed anybody." Following the Silver Rule means peace, but the Golden Rule means love.

Living by the Golden Rule means we treat others the way we want them to treat us. If we would like our spouse and children to be thoughtful of us, we must ask ourselves how thoughtful are we of them. I don't mean simply remembering to open the car door for your wife. Thoughtfulness requires *thought*. Take time to think: What can I do for my wife today? How can I help my son or daughter? How can I please my husband?

In the *House of the Golden Rule,* thoughtfulness reigns supreme. Every morning each member of the family greets one another with a smile and a hearty, "Good morning"— instead of, "Don't talk to me until I have had my coffee." Maybe you don't growl at your family in the morning, but does your lukewarm grunt indicate your indifference to their needs and feelings?

How about the way you depart the house for the day? Do you leave a flurry of smoldering hurts, angry feelings, and misunderstanding behind you? Or is your departure amidst warm hugs, loving words of encouragement, and sweet kisses? When the family *begins* the day right, the day *goes* right.

What about the return home? I think every husband should pray for wisdom and grace before he walks through the door. He needs to leave the burdens of the workplace behind him so he can face the challenges of homelife in love and peace. The wife also needs to prepare herself for the return of the husband. Her sensitivity to his needs can set the tone for the entire evening. How many evening meals have been ruined when mom started with, "You have to talk to Johnny! You wouldn't believe what he did today!" So everyone sits down at the table with tension and anxiety knotting in their stomachs. Not a very pleasant way to begin an evening at home.

Living to please others means you consider their needs above your own at that particular moment. Your home can become known as the house of the Golden Rule when you and your family learn to treat one another the way you want to be treated yourself—with thoughtfulness, kindness, and sensitivity.

The House On The Rock

Living by the Golden Rule as Jesus defined it may not be easy, but the results will transform your homelife. Jesus said, "Everyone who hears these words of mine and puts them

177

into practice is like the wise man who built his house on the rock. The rain came down, the streams rose, and the winds blew and beat against that house; yet it did not fall, because it had its foundation on the rock" (Matthew 7:24-25, *NIV*).

Those who ignore Jesus and build their lives on the things of this world will find that when the problems erode the foundation, their house will fall. How many people have lamented over their broken home? Yet they consistently ignored the teaching of God's Word about how to live with the people they love.

Jesus taught, "If you forgive men when they sin against you, your heavenly Father will also forgive you. But if you do not forgive men their sins, your Father will not forgive your sins" (Matthew 6:14-15, *NIV*). How many families ignore this teaching that is central to God's Word? Why is forgiveness so vital to healthy family relationships?

We are all sinners, and we all offend one another. That is why we must learn to forgive. When you are a porcupine living in a world of porcupines, your survival depends on how well you deal with the pricks. Forgiveness unlocks the door to healthy, happy relationships with the people we love. Do you wish your loved ones would overlook your faults and not hold them against you? Then you must forgive others when they make mistakes or harm you in any way.

John Wesley, the great revivalist of the nineteenth century, was traveling on a journey with a general and the general's servant. One day the servant, in a bumbling fashion, greatly offended his master. The general, a high-spirited man, told off the servant in no uncertain terms. When the servant implored him for forgiveness, the general snorted, "Forgive you! I never forgive anyone!" To this, John Wesley softly replied, "Then I hope, sir, that you never sin."

Why should we forgive? Because we ourselves have been forgiven. "Be ye kind one to another, tenderhearted, forgiving one another, even as God for Christ's sake hath forgiven you" (Ephesians 4:32).

In the gospel of Matthew, Peter asked Jesus how many times he should forgive his brother when he sins against him. Thinking that seven times was above and beyond the call of duty, Peter was hoping Jesus would supply a lower number. Instead, Jesus quoted a much higher figure, "Until seventy times seven" (Matthew 18:21-22). In other words, every time someone offends you, betrays you, criticizes you, hurts you, laughs at you, or does anything against you, your response should and must always be *to forgive*.

After preaching a sermon on forgiveness from the parable of the unforgiving servant (Matthew 18:21-35), I was stopped by a woman as she was leaving the church service. "Oh, how you have destroyed me!" she said.

"How is that?" I asked.

"There is a woman whom I cannot forgive. She once said to me, 'Go to hell,' and I can't forgive her for that."

"Jesus went to hell for you," I replied, "so we could be forgiven of our great debt of sin. How much more should we forgive others their offenses?"

A woman once read a letter written to her daughter by the girl's best friend. In this letter, the girlfriend wrote a comment about her friend's mother. The mother was greatly offended and forbade her daughter to ever allow her friend into the house again. As the years went by, the two girls remained friends by meeting secretly without the mother's knowledge. Finally, the pastor, who had heard about the incident, went to the mother and said, "Don't you think the time has come for you to forgive and invite your daughter's friend back into your home?" The mother looked up with great surprise and said, "Forgive her! Why, I forgave her years ago, but she still doesn't need to come in my house!"

How many of us deceive ourselves with that kind of thinking? "Oh, yes, I forgive him. But, I won't have anything to do with him." Suppose God said to you and me, "Yes, I will forgive your sins, but don't expect me to answer your prayers or take care of you." Forgiveness without reconciliation of the relationship is not forgiveness at all. Do you need to be reconciled to someone you love?

Jesus is the rock. If we build our lives and our families on Him and His teachings, we can control and improve the climate within our homes. Then our families will stand firm and secure in the midst of a turbulent generation and a storm-filled world.

What about the atmosphere in your home? Do you show the joy of Christ? Do you treat your children with love and affection? Is there a peaceful calm that brings serenity and security in the midst of a stress-filled society? A positive climate of love, joy, and peace in the home is one of the greatest gifts you can give your family.

Father, change the climate in our homes. Begin in our hearts as by faith we trust in Jesus Christ and allow the gentle breeze of His Spirit to cleanse and purify our lives. Teach us to forgive one another and show our love in word and deed by being thoughtful, kind, and concerned. May the sweet peace of Jesus and the joy of His love be the climate in which our children grow in body, soul, and spirit. In the name of Jesus Christ. Amen.

19

AS FOR ME AND MY HOUSE

You and your house. Have you ever considered that statement before? In our society, individuality and personal freedom often take precedence over family life. But that was not the case in Old Testament times. In those days, your family was you. The family unit was not just the basis of society—it *was* the society. If you didn't associate yourself with a family, you were a nobody. That's why lineage was so important—Abraham was the father of Isaac, who was the father of Jacob, who was the father of Joseph. . . .

Parents, and especially fathers, are responsible for determining the direction and purpose their families will take. One father in the Old Testament took this responsibility very seriously. When Joshua was near the end of his life, he assembled all the tribes of Israel together for one final message. In this farewell speech, he spoke the word of the Lord to the people. This passage helps us see the history of Israel from God's point of view. Particularly significant is the importance God attaches to the role of fathers.

"This is what the Lord, the God of Israel, says, 'Long ago your *forefathers,* including Terah the *father* of Abraham and Nahor, lived beyond the River and worshiped other Gods. But I took your *father* Abraham . . . and led him throughout Canaan and gave him many descendants. I gave him Isaac, and to Isaac I gave Jacob and Esau. . . .' " (Joshua 24:2-4, *NIV*, italics added). Then the Lord tells how He delivered the Israelites from Egypt and brought them back to the Promised Land, defeating their enemies and providing for their every need. It is at this point that Joshua makes his challenge to the people:

"Now fear the Lord and serve him with all faithfulness. Throw away the gods your *forefathers* worshiped beyond the River and in Egypt, and serve the Lord. But if serving the Lord seems undesirable to you, then choose for yourselves this day whom you will serve, whether the gods your *forefathers* served beyond the River, or the gods of the Amorites, in whose land you are living" (Joshua 24:14-15, *NIV*, italics added).

Then Joshua, as head of his family, makes this very bold statement: *"But as for me and my household, we will serve the Lord"* (verse 15). For over one hundred years this venerable old soldier-saint had personally witnessed the mighty power and protection of the Lord God of Israel. How could Joshua choose to serve anyone else?

As For Me

"As for *me*," he says. Deciding to serve God is always a personal decision because it involves the very heart of our being. "I will give you a new heart," says God, "and put a new spirit in you" (Ezekiel 36:26, *NIV*). Our whole person is transformed by the power of God's Holy Spirit. When we come to experience and know Jesus Christ as our own personal Savior, our life is changed. What can be more personal than that?

Have you ever heard someone say, "Oh, I don't like to talk about religion; it is too personal"? People often say that to me. But what they really mean, and which they are not willing to admit, is that they have nothing to talk about!

Although Joshua's decision was personal, it cannot be private. Jesus said, "Whoever acknowledges me before men I will also acknowledge him before my Father in heaven. But whoever disowns me before men, I will disown him before my Father in heaven'' (Matthew 10:32-33, *NIV*). Personal, yes; private, no.

Because it is such a personal decision, no one else can decide for you. Peter Marshall said, "There are no grandchildren in the family of God." How many people depend upon the religion of their parents or their grandparents, hoping that will save them? But there are no grandchildren in God's kingdom. We must all come to a personal experience with God ourselves.

Have you had that personal experience? Have you put your trust in Jesus Christ and asked Him to make all things new in your life? Do you know that your sins are forgiven and that God's Spirit dwells within you? People may see God in the stars or in the flowers, but unless they see Christ in the mirror on the wall, they have never really known Him at all. Do you have a personal relationship with Jesus Christ? This is the most important decision you will ever make.

Me And Mine

Joshua not only says "as for me" but "as for me and my household." Religion is not only personal; it is also a family affair. The course on which you set your family could be the one they take for generations. Look at the people of Israel. They were still worshiping the idols of their forefathers from centuries before. In spite of all that God had done for them, they had never made a conscious commitment to serve Him.

How many parents say, "Oh, we'll let our children choose their own religion when they grow up." Do these same parents say, "We will let our children decide, when they grow up, whether or not they want to go to school and learn to read and write"? Yet some parents are so foolish as to suppose that they can be neutral about religion.

My friends, there is no neutrality with God. If we do not teach our children to serve God, we are teaching them to serve Satan. Remember the words of Jesus: "If anyone causes one of these little ones who believe in me to sin, it would be better for him to have a large millstone hung around his neck and to be drowned in the depths of the sea" (Matthew 18:6, *NIV*). God holds *you* responsible for the spiritual choices that you make for your family.

Joshua said, "As for me and my household." That's a simple statement with tremendous overtones. If you had been in that position, what would you have said?

Would you have said, "My house *without me*"? Many husbands and fathers take that attitude toward Christianity and the church. But Joshua did not leave religion to the wife and children. He did not sing, "Take my *wife* and let her be, consecrated Lord to Thee." How about your house, gentlemen? Have you determined that not only your house but *you,* yourself, will serve the Lord? In your household, are you the one person the others are praying for—the one holdout—the one who has not given himself over to Jesus Christ?

Or maybe you would approach it from the other point of view and say, "As for me *without my house*." Do you have the self-righteous attitude of "just Jesus and me." Joshua was not so foolish. He made it clear that his family would be serving the Lord, too. No idols or worldly influences would be allowed in his home or on his property. He would do everything he could to teach his children the ways of God and bring them to a saving knowledge of Jesus Christ. Matthew Henry said, "If I can't bring as many as I would, I will bring as many as I can." And by the grace of God may that at least include the members of our families.

You could take the coward's way out and say, "As for me and my house, *if everybody else goes along*." Joshua boldly declared, "As for me and my house, in spite of what the rest of you do, we will serve the Lord." Joshua would not be led astray by the influence of others. Are you willing to stand alone and swim against the tide, regardless of what those around you decide to do? Many people are led astray or hindered in their service for God by the pernicious influence of friends and relatives who choose to serve the god of this world. "But everybody's doing it." That argument carried no weight with Joshua. If everybody in Israel were an idolater, Joshua and his household were going to serve the Lord—no matter what the consequences.

The Family Idol

Joshua's religion was personal; his religion involved his family; and his religion was practical. He said, "We will serve the Lord." He did not merely say, "We will make a profession," but he boldly declared, "We will serve the Lord."

What is God's purpose for your home and family? Have you ever asked yourself that question? Why did God place men, women, boys, and girls in families? Joshua knew the answer: To serve God and glorify Him through their lives.

Some people have a false conception concerning this matter of serving the Lord as a household. They proclaim, (although they would never say it verbally), "As for me and my house, *we will serve ourselves*." That is the ultimate idolatry—selfishness. Yet many families have the attitude of "me, my wife, and my son John. Just we three, no more." Idolatry! Unrecognized idolatry!

Because of the increase in broken homes, a great deal of emphasis has been placed on family life and doing things together. That is great, but some people have overreacted and gone overboard. Satan always moves from one extreme to another. If we do not keep our priorities in proper perspective, the family itself can become an idol. If we retreat into our homes, providing only for ourselves without sharing our lives and love with others, selfishness will destroy us.

Some Christians have adopted the attitude expressed in this take-off on a familiar song: "We'll build a sweet little nest, somewhere out in the west, and let the rest of the world go to hell!'' If that is your family's theme song, then you are treading on dangerous ground. God has a way of casting down man-made idols. Don't think He will allow you to worship at the altar of family togetherness while His heart is breaking for a lost and dying world. Jesus Christ left His home in heaven to come to earth to die for you. Will you not offer your home and family in service to Him?

Who's Serving Who?

Other people proclaim, "As for me and my house, *the Lord will serve us.*" That is a very subtle distortion, and I hear various overtones of it all the time: "What is it going to do for me?" "What can your church do for our family?" When it comes to accepting Jesus Christ, their first questions are, "Must I give up this?" or "Must I give up that to be a Christian?" If they were sincere, their first question would be, "What can I give up for the sake of Jesus Christ who gave up His life for me?" Which is the attitude of your heart?

Many people simply cast their intellectual vote in God's direction, but their heart's vote is still with the world. My friends, a true profession of faith in Jesus Christ involves a belief that God is infinitely superior to anything in this world. Salvation involves giving up the spoils of this world and its worldly pleasures for Jesus Christ and what He offers. "Love not the world, neither the things that are in the world. If any man love the world, the love of the Father is not in him" (1 John 2:15). No man can serve two masters.

Some Christians have a negative view of Christianity that involves simply not doing this, not doing that, and not doing the other thing, rather than doing something positive. They think if they keep their noses clean, stay away from ungodly people, and avoid the evil in the world, that makes them good Christians. By replacing the condemned sins of the world with acceptable pleasures, they continue to live a hedonistic, selfish lifestyle.

Serving God and others is the other side of the coin, but some people never bother to turn it over and see what it says. They never take the time to find out what the Bible says God expects from them. If you view Christianity simply as a cure all for your family's ills, you will be sadly disappointed. The power of God can only work in your homelife when you have made a complete and committed surrender of yourself and your selfish ways to the cross of Jesus Christ.

We Will Serve The Lord

"As for me and my house, we will *say* that we serve the Lord." Our churches are full of people who make this profession. The same was true in Joshua's day. When he put forth his bold challenge, the people of Israel were very quick to say, "Far be it from us to forsake the Lord to serve other gods. . . . We too will serve the Lord, because he is our God" (Joshua 24:16-18, *NIV*).

But what happened after Joshua and the people of his generation had died? "After that . . . another generation grew up, who knew neither the Lord nor what he had done for Israel. Then the Israelites did evil in the eyes of the Lord and served the Baals. They forsook the Lord, the God of their fathers" (Judges 2:10-12, *NIV*).

How could that happen within such a short period of time? How could an entire generation grow up and not know God and all He had done for Israel? Because their parents didn't tell them. They had *said* they would serve the Lord, but they had neglected the most important part of service: teaching their children about God.

You can say you serve the Lord by going to church, tithing, singing in the choir, teaching Sunday school, etc.; but if you are failing to teach your children God's ways at home, all your religious duties are in vain. Many professing Christians say, "Oh, yes, me and my house, we will serve the Lord." They say it, but they do not do it. And God says that their faith is vain. Andrew Murray wrote, "God does not want to be worshiped without being served." Are you and your household truly serving the Lord?

It was an inspiration to me to visit in the home of Art DeMoss and witness the commitment of mother, father, and children to the great cause of Jesus Christ. About five days after Art died, I received a letter he had written before his death. In that letter he told about a dinner party he and his wife had had in their home just a few days before. One hundred and seventy-eight people accepted Jesus Christ as Savior that night. The month before, over a hundred and seventy-five people had made the same decision in meetings at Art's home. Over the years, thousands of others came to the Lord through the ministry of this home committed to serving the Lord. Art DeMoss was a modern Joshua.

I praise God for homes that have been given over to the service of the Lord. A family in our own church turned their home into a "greenhouse" where tender young lives could come and grow in the Lord. As a result, hundreds of young people have come to know the Savior and have gone forth to serve Him.

My friends, what is the example of your home? Are you serving the Lord? Is there a positive influence and a determined effort to make your home a beacon of light in a world dying without Jesus Christ? May God inscribe these words on our hearts and on our homes: *Regardless of what other men may do, as for me and my house, we will serve the Lord.*

Heavenly Father, we commit our homes and families to You and Your service. Help us in the events of daily life to choose to serve You before ourselves and our own selfish desires. May our homes be a place where the lost can find You, the hungry can be fed, and the weak can be strengthened. We yield our lives and our households over to Your service. Take us and use us for Your glory. In the name of Jesus Christ, our Savior and Lord. Amen.

SUGGESTED READING

Adams, Jay E. *Christian Living in the Home* (Grand Rapids, Michigan: Baker Book House, 1972).

Drakeford, John W. *Marriage: How to Keep a Good Thing Growing* (Nashville, Tennessee: Impact Books/The Benson Company, 1979).

Engelsma, David. *Marriage: The Mystery of Christ and The Church* (Grand Rapids, Michigan: Reformed Free Publishing Association, 1975).

Evans, Dr. Louis H. *Your Marriage: Duel or Duet?* (Westwood, New Jersey: Fleming H. Revell Company, 1962).

Henry, Dr. Joseph B. *Fulfillment in Marriage* (Westwood, New Jersey: Fleming H. Revell Company, 1966)

LaHaye, Tim and Beverly. *The Act of Marriage* (Grand Rapids, Michigan: Zondervan Publishing House, 1976).

Lovette, C. S. *Unequally Yoked Wives* (Baldwin Park, California: Personal Christianity, 1968).

Murray, Andrew. *How to Bring Your Children to Christ* (Springdale, Pennsylvania: Whitaker House, 1984).

Powell, John. *Why Am I Afraid to Tell You Who I Am?* (Niles, Illinois: Argus Communications, 1969).

Wheat, Ed. *Love Life For Every Married Couple* (Grand Rapids, Michigan: Zondervan Publishing House, 1980).